FAST FIXES FOR ALMOST
EVERYTHING
AROUND YOUR HOUSE

Plumbing • Heating and Cooling
Wiring • Lighting • Appliance

Charlie Wing

Reader's Digest

The Reader's Digest Association, Inc.
Pleasantville, NY

Library of Congress Cataloging in Publication Data:
ISBN 13: 978-0-7621-0850-3
ISBN 10: 0-7621-0850-9

Address any comments to:
The Reader's Digest Association, Inc.
Adult Trade Publishing
Reader's Digest Road
Pleasantville, NY 10570-7000

For more Reader's Digest products and information, visit our website:

rd.com (in the United States)

Printed in China

1 3 5 7 9 10 8 6 4 2

This title was previously published as *Smart Homeowner's Pocket Guide to Home
System Repairs*. The information in this book is derived from *The Big Book of Small
Household Repairs* by Charlie Wing.

WARNING
All do-it-yourself activities involve a degree of risk. Skills, materials, tools, and
site conditions vary widely. Although the editors have made every effort to ensure
accuracy, the reader remains responsible for the selection and use of tools, materials,
and methods. Always obey local codes and laws, follow the manufacturer's operating
instructions, and observe safety precautions.

Contents

Wiring

Heating and Cooling

CONTENTS

INTRODUCTION:
FIXING THE SMALL STUFF

The majority of homeowners, even smart homeowners, live lives of quiet resignation, hostage to myriad minor, yet aggravating, home defects. Since these problems seem too small to warrant the attention of $50-$100 per-hour professionals, the defects persist. Why don't we fix them ourselves? Usually because we're convinced only professional tradespeople possess the skills and arcane knowledge required to not botch the job. If you are one of these homeowners, you are in good company. Let me tell you a story.

A few years back, I was visiting a friend who happened to be a professional plumber. The doorbell rang, and there appeared an appliance repairman, replete with intimidating tool belt and massive service manual. He was there, in answer to my friend's call, to repair the dishwasher. I assumed there was something terribly wrong with the appliance. Otherwise my plumber friend would never have agreed to the minimum charge of $125.

"The machine makes a weird whizzing sound, like the motor bearings are gone," my friend said.

Without a word, the repairman plucked a simple Phillips screwdriver from his tool belt and unscrewed the perforated cover of the dishwasher's drain. He reached in with two fingers and held up a pecan shell. "Here is your culprit," he beamed.

He replaced the drain cover and turned on the machine. The noise had disappeared. "That will be $125," the serviceman said.

Reader's Digest and I hope this little book saves you many hundreds of dollars. Keep it at hand in your toolbox.

—Charlie Wing

PLUMBING

ADJUSTING A SINK POP-UP DRAIN

*Most of the bathroom sink pop-up stoppers in the
world have stopped working. Either they won't
stay open or closed, or they leak. That is because
their owners have never looked under the sink.
Amaze your friends and family by fixing yours.*

1. If the stopper doesn't pop up when the pull control is pushed down, pinch the spring clip with slip-joint pliers and move the pivot rod down one hole in the clevis. Alternatively, loosen the clevis screw with the slip-joint pliers, pull the clevis down until the stopper pops up, and tighten the clevis screw again.

2. If the stopper won't hold water even when closed, remove the stopper by lifting it straight up, or by turning it and lifting it. If it still won't release, remove the retaining nut with groove-joint pliers, pull the pivot rod out, and pull the stopper up. Clean the stopper seal or, if worn, replace it.

3. If the stopper won't remain in either the closed or the open position, tighten the retaining nut with groove-joint pliers until it will.

4. If water leaks from the pivot ball, remove the retaining nut with groove-joint pliers. Pull out the pivot rod, gasket and washer—if there is one. Take the gasket and washer to the hardware store and purchase identical replacements. Reassemble the pivot assembly.

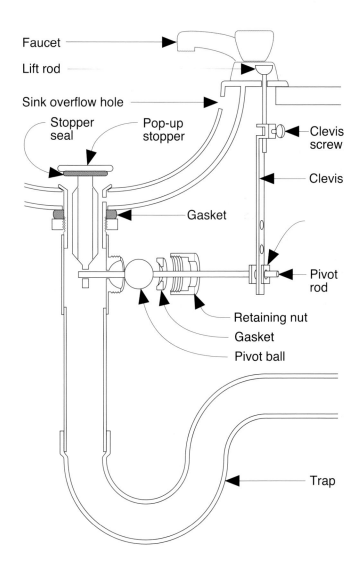

Faucet

Lift rod

Sink overflow hole

Stopper seal

Pop-up stopper

Clevis screw

Clevis

Gasket

Pivot rod

Retaining nut

Gasket

Pivot ball

Trap

REPLACING A KITCHEN SINK STRAINER

If your sink strainer won't hold water, try replacing the strainer basket first. Take the old one to a home center to find a similar replacement for less than $5. If the strainer leaks, replace the entire assembly as described below.

1. Loosen the two slip nuts from the tailpiece by turning them counterclockwise with the groove-joint pliers.

2. Slide the tailpiece down into the trap, or if in the way, remove the tailpiece. In either case, save the slip nuts and their washers.

3. Remove the locknut by turning it counterclockwise with a spud wrench. If it refuses to turn, tap gently on the wrench handle with a claw hammer.

4. Remove the friction ring and rubber gasket from beneath, then push the strainer up through the sink.

5. Clean all of the old putty or other sealant from the rim of the sinkhole using a putty knife.

6. Coat the flange of the new strainer with plumber's putty and insert the strainer into the sink.

7. From below, place the rubber gasket and friction ring over the strainer, then thread and tighten the new locknut.

8. Place the top plastic washer over the tailpiece, slide the tailpiece up to the strainer, and tighten the top slip nut. Tighten the lower slip nut onto the trap.

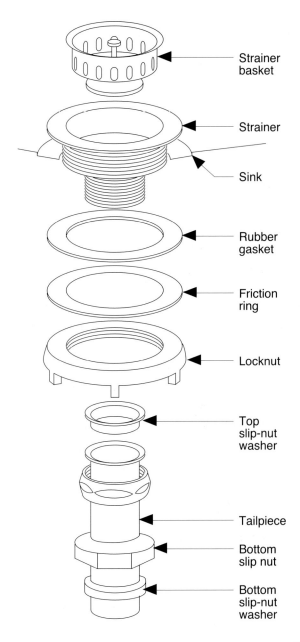

Strainer
basket

Strainer

Sink

Rubber
gasket

Friction
ring

Locknut

Top
slip-nut
washer

Tailpiece

Bottom
slip nut

Bottom
slip-nut
washer

Unclogging a Sink Drain

The best time to unclog a sink drain is before the drain becomes completely blocked. Commercial drain cleaners will usually remove accumulated grease and hair. If the blockage becomes complete, the steps below will cure it.

1. Remove the pop-up stopper if there is one. Most stoppers lift out, or will after they are turned.

2. If the stopper will not lift out, place a bucket under the trap, remove the retaining nut with groove-joint pliers, and pull the pivot rod straight back (Fig. A). Now lift the stopper.

3. Draw 4 inches of water in the sink.

4. Stuff the sink overflow with a washcloth or rag.

5. While a helper holds the washcloth in place, place a plunger over the drain and give it a dozen vigorous vertical plunges.

6. If Step 5 doesn't succeed, loosen the two slip nuts on the trap with groove-joint pliers and remove the trap.

7. Cut a wire coat hanger with diagonal-cutting pliers and bend a hook in one end. Use the hook to fish the blockage out of the tailpiece, the trap or the drainpipe.

8. If Step 7 didn't succeed, call the plumber.

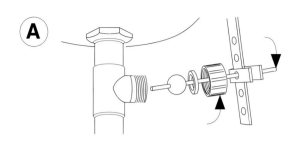

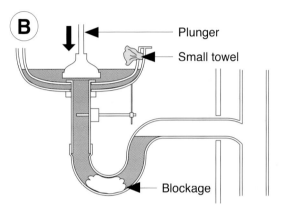

Plunger

Small towel

Blockage

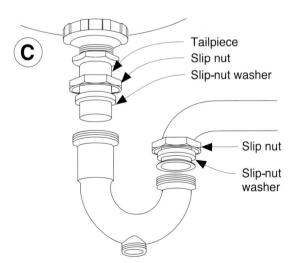

Tailpiece
Slip nut
Slip-nut washer

Slip nut

Slip-nut washer

REPLACING A SINK SPRAY

If you have already cleaned the perforated disk in your sink spray head and it still malfunctions, replace the entire spray head/hose assembly. The whole assembly costs about $10.

1. Clean out under the sink and place a towel under the faucet assembly to catch water.

2. Remove the hose coupling under the faucet by turning it counterclockwise with a basin wrench. If you don't have a basin wrench, try locking pliers.

3. Grab the spray head and pull the entire hose assembly up through the spray head holder.

4. With your fingers, apply pipe-joint compound to the threads of the hose nipple.

5. Thread a new spray hose through the spray head holder and screw the hose coupling clockwise onto the hose nipple.

6. Turn on the sink faucet and operate the spray head.

7. Check under the sink for leaks. Tighten the hose coupling further, if necessary.

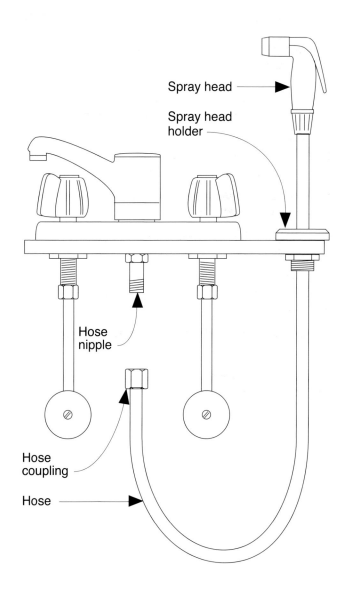

Spray head

Spray head
holder

Hose
nipple

Hose
coupling

Hose

REPLACING A BATHROOM SINK

An inexpensive way to modernize your bathroom is to replace the sink and toilet. Unlike toilets, bathroom sinks come in a wide variety of shapes and sizes. To avoid having to replace the vanity top as well, make sure the new sink cutout is the same size as the old cutout, and that the faucet centerset has the same hole spacing.

1. Look under the sink for any sink clips (Fig. A). If there are any, remove them by turning the screws counterclockwise with a screwdriver. It is not necessary to remove the screws.

2. Turn off the supply valves under the sink. If there are no supply valves under the sink, look for shutoff valves in the basement. If necessary, shut off the main supply valve near the water meter.

3. Loosen both bottom supply slip nuts with an adjustable wrench (Fig. B).

4. Loosen the drain slip nut with a pipe wrench.

5. Lift the sink straight up and place it upside down.

6. Loosen the drain locknut with the pipe wrench and remove the sink strainer and tailpiece. You may have to keep the strainer from twisting by inserting slip-joint plier handles from the other side.

7. Remove the faucet locknuts with the adjustable wrench and remove the faucet.

8. Purchase a new sink that requires the same or larger counter cutout and the same spacing between the faucet supply holes. Enlarge the countertop cutout, if necessary, with a keyhole or sabre saw.

(continued on page 12)

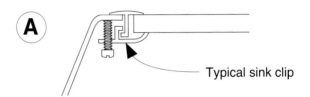

A

Typical sink clip

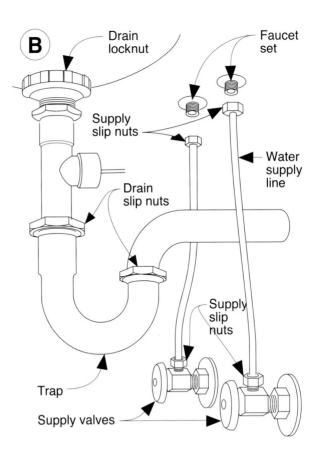

B

Drain locknut

Faucet set

Supply slip nuts

Water supply line

Drain slip nuts

Supply slip nuts

Trap

Supply valves

9. Apply plumber's putty to the base of the faucet centerset (Fig. C), insert the faucet set into the holes in the sink, and fasten it with the supply lock-nuts using an adjustable wrench.

10. With your fingers, apply plumber's putty to the flange of the new drain assembly (Fig. D), insert the assembly into the sink drain hole, and fasten it with the drain locknut using the pipe wrench.

11. Apply clear silicone sealant under the sink rim, lower the sink into the countertop cutout, and reat-tach the sink clips, if any.

12. Slide the lift rod down through the hole in the centerset.

13. Squeezing the spring clip with your fingers, slide the pivot rod through the spring clip and one of the clevis holes (Fig. E).

14. Attach the supply pipes with the bottom sup-ply nuts.

15. Slide the trap up over the bottom of the drain tailpiece and tighten the drain slip nut.

16. Turn on the water supply and check both the drain and the supply pipes for leaks.

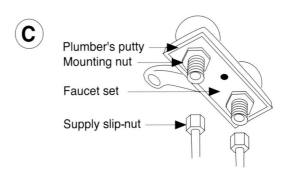

C

Plumber's putty
Mounting nut

Faucet set

Supply slip-nut

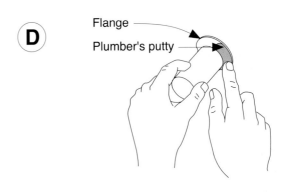

D

Flange
Plumber's putty

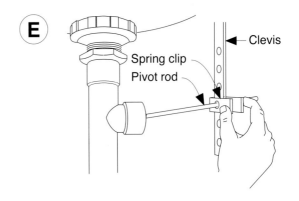

E

Clevis
Spring clip
Pivot rod

CLEANING A FAUCET AERATOR

If you have your own water supply or if your water main has been worked on recently, your faucet aerator screen may have collected some debris. Removing the screen is a simple task. If the screen becomes clogged very often, consider leaving it out; no harm will be done.

1. Wrap several turns of masking tape around the aerator. Alternatively, hold a rubber jar opener around the aerator.

2. Grip the protected aerator with groove-joint pliers and unscrew it counterclockwise.

3. Disassemble the aerator and lay the parts out in order.

4. If there are any mineral deposits on the perforated disk and screen, soak both overnight in vinegar.

5. Remove any other material blocking the screen or disk with a toothpick.

6. Reassemble the aerator and screw it back on, protecting the surface as before.

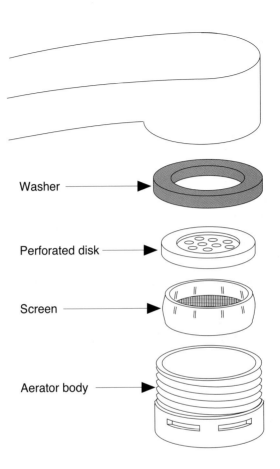

Washer

Perforated disk

Screen

Aerator body

REPAIRING A ROTATING BALL FAUCET

If your single-lever faucet has a round cap just under the handle, it is probably a ball-type faucet. If the faucet is dripping, tighten the cap clockwise with groove-joint pliers before going any further.

1. Turn off the water supply.

2. Find an Allen wrench that fits snugly into the setscrew in the handle and turn the setscrew counterclockwise until the handle lifts off.

3. Grip the knurled ring of the cap with groove-joint pliers and remove it by turning counterclockwise.

4. Remove the cam, rubber cam seal and ball.

5. With a small screwdriver, lift out the neoprene seals and springs.

6. Remove the spout by twisting and lifting at the same time.

7. Remove the O-rings.

8. Place the cam, cam seal, ball, neoprene seals, springs and O-rings in a plastic zipper bag, and take them to a hardware store to find a kit with matching parts.

9. Coat the new O-rings with waterproof grease and seat them in their grooves.

10. Install the remaining replacement parts. If the ball contains a slot, align the slot with the pin in the body. Fit the tab on the cam into the notch in the body before screwing down the cap.

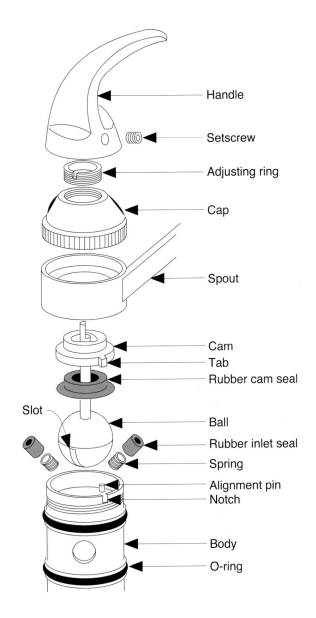

Handle

Setscrew

Adjusting ring

Cap

Spout

Cam

Tab

Rubber cam seal

Slot

Ball

Rubber inlet seal

Spring

Alignment pin

Notch

Body

O-ring

REPAIRING A CARTRIDGE FAUCET

The majority of single-lever—and some double-lever—faucets are of the cartridge type. There are dozens of cartridge styles, so don't forget to take the old cartridge to the home center to find a replacement. The color of the replacement cartridge doesn't matter—just the construction.

1. Turn off the water supply.

2. If there is a cap covering the handle screw, pry it off with a small screwdriver.

3. Remove the handle screw with a screwdriver.

4. Remove the handle by lifting it straight up.

5. Remove the plastic retaining nut with groove-joint pliers.

6. If there is a clip retaining the cartridge, remove it with the small screwdriver or long-nose pliers.

7. Remove the spout by twisting it and lifting it at the same time.

8. Remove the large O-rings from the faucet body with the small screwdriver.

9. Grip the cartridge stem with slip-joint pliers and pull straight up.

10. Take the cartridge and O-rings to the hardware store and purchase replacements.

11. Coat the new O-rings with waterproof grease and seat them in their grooves.

12. Replace the remaining parts in the order opposite to disassembly. If the cartridge has either a tab or a flat surface, make sure it faces forward.

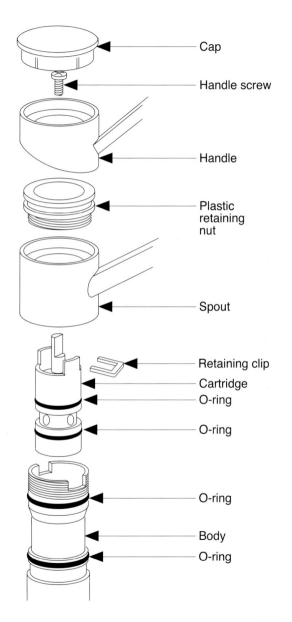

Cap

Handle screw

Handle

Plastic
retaining
nut

Spout

Retaining clip

Cartridge

O-ring

O-ring

O-ring

Body

O-ring

Repairing a Disk Faucet

The cartridge in a disk-type faucet rarely wears out. Try cleaning the neoprene seals and the inlet holes before purchasing an expensive replacement cartridge. Also, remember to move the handle to the "On" position before turning the water supply back on to avoid damaging the cartridge.

1. Turn off the water supply.

2. Locate the setscrew in the handle and find either an Allen wrench or a screwdriver that will fit. Loosen the setscrew and remove both the handle and the escutcheon.

3. Remove the screws in the top of the cartridge, then lift the cartridge straight up and out.

4. Take the cartridge to a hardware store and purchase exact replacements for the three tiny rubber seals in the bottom of the cartridge. Replace the cartridge only if it continues leaking after replacement of the seals.

5. Using a small screwdriver, remove the old seals, clean out the holes they were seated in, and install the new seals.

6. Line the cartridge seals up with the holes in the faucet body, and install the cartridge.

7. Replace the cap and handle.

8. Move the handle to the "On" position.

9. Turn on the water supply valves.

10. As soon as the water runs steadily, move the handle to the "Off" position.

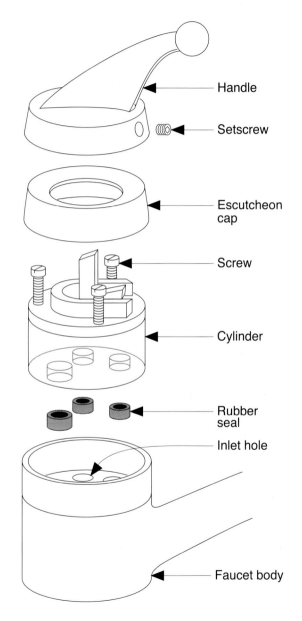

Handle

Setscrew

Escutcheon
cap

Screw

Cylinder

Rubber
seal

Inlet hole

Faucet body

REPAIRING A COMPRESSION FAUCET

Replacing the washer in a faucet is the classic home repair. This is not because it is difficult, but because it has to be done so often and because there are so many different washer sizes. To make the job simple, take the threaded spindle with you to the hardware store to make sure the O-ring, stem washer and stem screw are all exactly the right size.

1. Turn off the water supply.

2. Pry off the handle cap with a small screwdriver.

3. Remove the handle by turning its screw counterclockwise and lifting.

4. Remove the stem assembly by turning the packing nut counterclockwise with an adjustable wrench.

5. Separate the stem and packing nut.

6. Take the stem to a hardware store and purchase identical stem washer, stem screw and O-ring. Purchase packing string if the packing nut contains packing.

7. Install the new seat washer and screw.

8. Install the new O-ring and screw the stem into the packing nut. If the stem has packing instead, dig out the old packing and wind new packing around the stem inside the packing nut until nearly full.

9. Turn the stem to retract the washer.

10. Insert the stem assembly and tighten the packing nut with adjustable pliers.

11. Turn on the water supply and shut the faucet. If the faucet still leaks, try tightening the packing nut further. Otherwise, install a new valve seat. (See "Replacing a Worn Valve Seat" on page 24.)

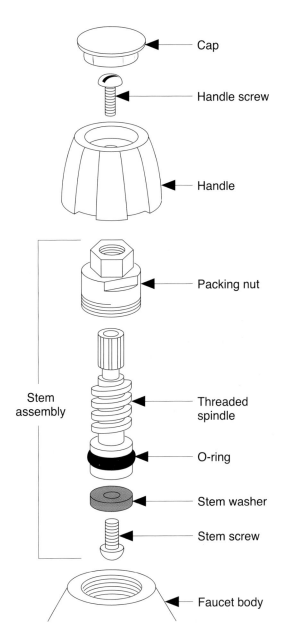

Cap

Handle screw

Handle

Packing nut

Stem
assembly

Threaded
spindle

O-ring

Stem washer

Stem screw

Faucet body

REPLACING A WORN VALVE SEAT

If your faucet chews up washers more than once per year, it may have a damaged or corroded valve seat. Fortunately, the seat is replaceable. You can tell if the seat is damaged by inserting and twisting your forefinger in the faucet body.

1. Turn off the water supply.

2. If the handle has a cap, pry it off with a small screwdriver.

3. Remove the handle by turning its screw counterclockwise and lifting.

4. Remove the stem assembly by turning the hexagonal packing nut counterclockwise with an adjustable wrench.

5. Find a large Allen wrench that will fit snugly in the hexagonal hole in the valve seat. Alternatively, purchase a valve-seat wrench. Turn the wrench counterclockwise and remove the old valve seat.

6. Take the old valve seat to the hardware store and purchase an exact replacement.

7. Install the new valve seat with the same wrench used to remove the old one.

8. Turn the stem counterclockwise to retract the washer.

9. Insert the stem assembly and tighten the packing nut with the adjustable wrench.

10. Turn on the water supply and shut off the faucet. If the faucet still leaks, try tightening the packing nut further.

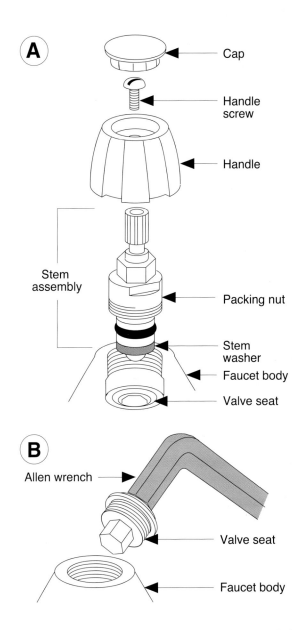

A

Cap

Handle screw

Handle

Stem assembly

Packing nut

Stem washer

Faucet body

Valve seat

B

Allen wrench

Valve seat

Faucet body

Replacing a Water-Filter Cartridge

Water-filter cartridges are inexpensive and marvelous at removing sediment and bad taste from drinking water. Eventually, however, they become totally blocked by the impurities they remove and require replacement. You should replace filter cartridges every few months—even if the water still flows easily—because they can become breeding grounds for bacteria.

1. Place a bucket under the filter.

2. Turn off the shutoff valve to the filter (Fig. A). On some models the valve is built into the filter. If you cannot find a shutoff valve, turn off the main valve.

3. If there is a pressure-release button in the cap, press it (Fig. A).

4. Grab the housing in both hands and unscrew it. If the housing will not turn, use an automotive oil-filter wrench to loosen it (Fig. A).

5. Remove the cartridge (Fig. B) and take it with you when you purchase a replacement cartridge of the same type.

6. Wash out the filter housing with a sponge and chlorine bleach.

7. If the replacement cartridge package contains an O-ring, coat the ring lightly with petroleum jelly and replace the old O-ring.

8. Place the new cartridge in the housing—either end up—and screw the housing clockwise onto the cap. Do not use the oil-filter wrench to tighten; tighten the housing only hand-tight.

9. Turn on the water supply and check for leaks. Tighten the housing further if necessary.

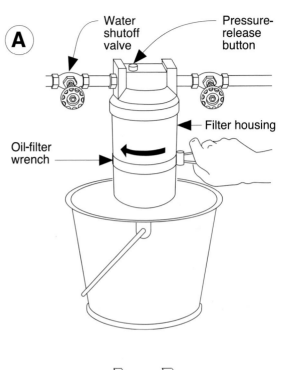

A

Water shutoff valve

Pressure-release button

Filter housing

Oil-filter wrench

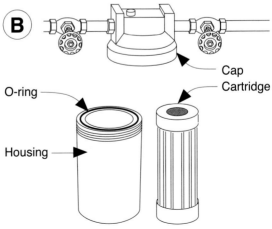

B

Cap

Cartridge

O-ring

Housing

REPAIRING A FREEZE-PROOF FAUCET

A freeze-proof sillcock is similar to a common hose bib except that it has an extra-long stem reaching back to the stem washer about 12 inches inside the house. Like any other faucet, it requires periodic replacement of the stem washer.

1. Turn off the shutoff valve to the sillcock inside the house. If you cannot find the shutoff, turn off the main shutoff valve, which should be next to the water meter.

2. Remove the sillcock handle screw and then the handle.

3. With an adjustable wrench, remove the hexagonal retaining nut by turning it counterclockwise.

4. Turn the stem counterclockwise and pull the stem all the way out.

5. Take the retaining nut and the stem to a hardware store and purchase replacement O-rings and a stem washer.

6. Replace the O-rings and washer.

7. Insert the stem and turn it clockwise as far as it will go.

8. Screw on the hexagonal nut with the adjustable wrench.

9. Replace the handle and secure it with the screw.

10. Turn the water back on and check for leaks.

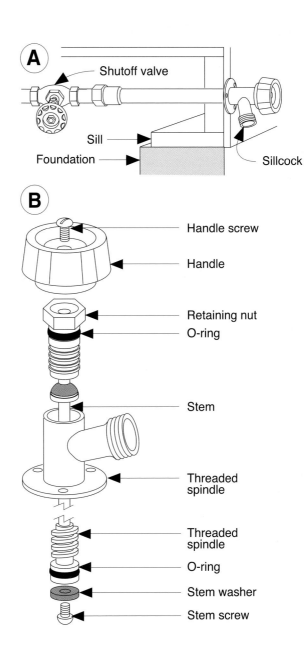

A

Shutoff valve

Sill

Foundation

Sillcock

B

Handle screw

Handle

Retaining nut

O-ring

Stem

Threaded spindle

Threaded spindle

O-ring

Stem washer

Stem screw

Repairing a Hose Bib

A hose bib is a faucet with a threaded spout for the connection of garden hoses and appliances such as clothes washers. If the bib is leaking from the handle, try tightening the packing nut with an adjustable wrench before disassembly.

1. Turn off the shutoff valve to the hose bib inside the house. If you cannot find the shutoff, turn off the main valve, which should be next to the water meter.

2. Remove the handle screw and handle.

3. Remove the hexagonal packing nut by turning it counterclockwise with an adjustable wrench.

4. Turn the stem counterclockwise and lift it out.

5. Take the stem and the packing nut to the hardware store and purchase replacements for the packing—either a packing washer or packing string—and the stem washer and screw.

6. Replace the stem washer and screw.

7. Insert the packing washer and packing ring into the packing nut and insert the stem. If the packing nut contains packing string instead, dig out the old string, insert the stem into the nut, and wind new packing string around the stem until the cavity in the nut is nearly full.

8. Insert the stem assembly into the faucet body and tighten the packing nut.

9. Replace the handle and turn it off.

10. Turn the supply back on. If the bib still leaks, tighten the packing nut further.

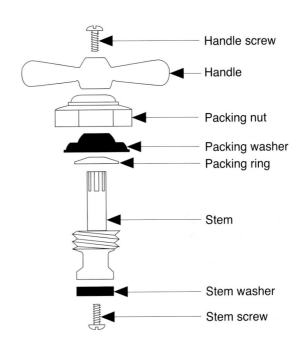

Handle screw

Handle

Packing nut

Packing washer

Packing ring

Stem

Stem washer

Stem screw

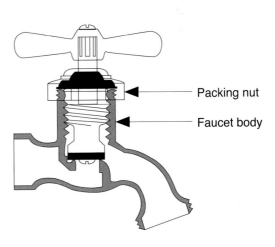

Packing nut

Faucet body

REPAIRING A SHOWERHEAD

Heating water is expensive—especially if you do it electrically. For less than $10, a water-saving showerhead can be a repair that pays for itself.

1. Place masking tape over the jaws of an adjustable wrench and remove the entire showerhead by turning the swivel-ball nut counterclockwise.

2. If you are replacing the showerhead because the spray has become erratic or because it leaks, you can fix it with Steps 3 through 6. If you want to replace the head, proceed to Step 7.

3. Use groove-joint pliers wrapped in masking tape to remove the collar nut.

4. Clean out both inlet and outlet holes with a straightened paper clip. If the deposit buildup is severe, soak the showerhead in vinegar overnight.

5. If the O-ring is worn, replace it with an identical size from the hardware store.

6. Assemble the showerhead.

7. Apply pipe-joint sealant to the threads of the shower arm and screw on the head.

8. Turn the water on. If the head leaks at the swivel, tighten the collar nut; if at the arm, tighten the swivel-ball nut.

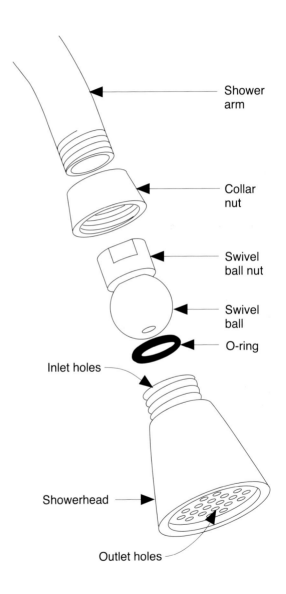

Shower
arm

Collar
nut

Swivel
ball nut

Swivel
ball

O-ring

Inlet holes

Showerhead

Outlet holes

UNCLOGGING A SHOWER DRAIN

Do you find yourself standing in a puddle every time you shower? If so, your shower drain is becoming clogged. Forestall trouble by using drain cleaner before the blockage becomes complete. If the drain does become totally blocked, here are two simple ways to clear it.

1. Spread the prongs of a pair of long-nose pliers, insert them into the holes of the shower strainer, and either flip the strainer out or twist it counter-clockwise to unscrew it (Fig. A).

2. Fill the shower base to a depth of about 1 inch—if it isn't already!

3. Place a plunger over the drain, and plunge up and down forcefully (Fig. B).

4. If Step 3 didn't clear the drain, remove the nozzle from a garden hose and insert the hose as far as you can into the drain.

5. Wrap a dishtowel or small hand towel tightly around the hose and stuff it into the drain (Fig. C).

6. Connect the hose to a hose bib.

7. Crimp the hose and open the valve.

8. While a helper holds the towel firmly in place, quickly crimp and uncrimp the hose, giving the drain short blasts of water.

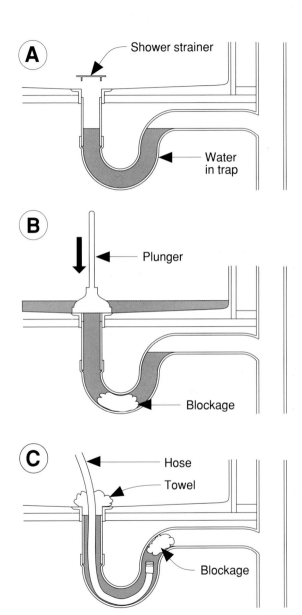

A   Shower strainer

Water in trap

B   Plunger

Blockage

C   Hose

Towel

Blockage

CLEANING A POP-UP TUB DRAIN

Because we shampoo in our tubs, a lot of long hair gets flushed down and remains in the drain. Unfortunately, hair is easily caught and seems to last forever. However, the pop-up style of drain is simple to pop out completely to allow cleaning.

1. Flip the drain lever up to pop the drain stopper up and pull the stopper completely out of the drain.

2. With a screwdriver, remove the screws from the overflow cover plate and pull the drain assembly (Fig. B) out of the overflow hole.

3. Remove the accumulated material from all of the parts and scrub the parts with a toothbrush and vinegar.

4. If the tub drains slowly with the drain assembly removed, feed a hand auger into the overflow opening and down through the drain.

5. When there is resistance, start turning the auger clockwise and withdraw it slowly. With luck, the clogging material will be hooked on the auger. Repeat Steps 4 and 5 until the tub drains normally.

6. Insert the drain assembly (Fig. B) through the overflow hole and replace the cover plate.

7. Flip the drain lever up and insert the stopper assembly into the drain.

8. If the tub now either drains slowly or will not hold water, withdraw the drain assembly and adjust the position of the threaded rod and nut at the top of the linkage with an adjustable wrench: shorter to speed draining, longer to stop leaking.

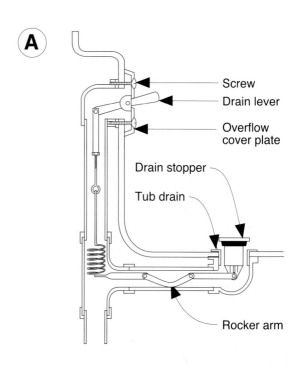

(A)

Screw

Drain lever

Overflow cover plate

Drain stopper

Tub drain

Rocker arm

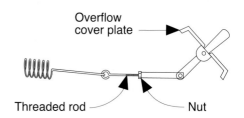

(B) DRAIN ASSEMBLY

Overflow cover plate

Threaded rod

Nut

CLEANING A PLUNGER-TYPE TUB DRAIN

A pop-up drain often clogs with hair so that the water drains slowly or not at all. A plunger-type tub drain has the opposite problem—hair may prevent its fully closing so that it does not hold water. Fortunately, it is simple to disassemble and clean.

1. Remove the screws holding the overflow cover plate (Fig. A).

2. Pull the entire drain assembly—cover plate, linkage and plunger—out of the tub (Fig. B).

3. Clean the linkage and plunger with vinegar and a toothbrush, then dry and smear the plunger with petroleum jelly.

4. If the tub drains slowly with the drain assembly removed, feed a hand auger into the overflow opening and down through the drain.

5. When there is resistance, start turning the auger clockwise and withdraw it slowly. With luck, the clogging material will be hooked on the auger. Repeat Steps 4 and 5 until the tub drains normally.

6. Insert the drain assembly (Fig. B) through the overflow opening and replace the cover plate.

7. If the tub now either drains slowly or will not hold water, withdraw the drain assembly and adjust the position of the threaded rod and nut at the top of the linkage with an adjustable wrench: shorter to speed draining, longer to stop leaking.

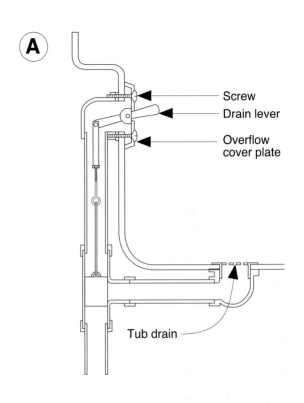

A

Screw
Drain lever
Overflow cover plate

Tub drain

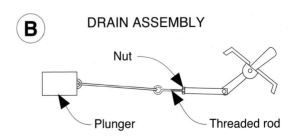

B DRAIN ASSEMBLY

Nut

Plunger

Threaded rod

ADJUSTING A TOILET HANDLE

*If your toilet tank doesn't flush easily and complete-
ly when you push down on the handle, chances
are the handle or the lifting wires or chains
attached to the handle need tightening. This is the
simplest of toilet repairs, requiring no new materials or parts.*

1. If the tank handle seems floppy, tighten the nut
inside the tank by turning it counterclockwise with
an adjustable wrench. Note that the direction is
opposite that of a usual nut.

2. If the handle lever is connected to a lift chain and
you have to hold the handle down to make the toilet
flush completely, shorten the chain by hooking it farther down (Fig. A). It should have slack of $1/2$ inch
when the stopper is in its normal, closed position.

3. If the handle lever connects to a lift wire and
you have to hold the handle down for a complete
flush, bend the upper, right-angled lift wire to lift
the stopper farther (Fig. B).

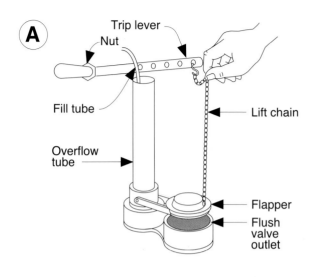

A

Trip lever

Nut

Fill tube

Overflow tube

Lift chain

Flapper

Flush valve outlet

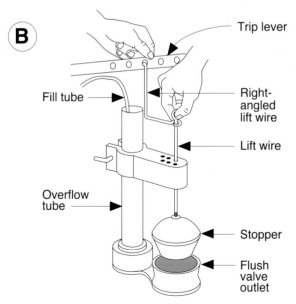

B

Trip lever

Fill tube

Right-angled lift wire

Lift wire

Overflow tube

Stopper

Flush valve outlet

ADJUSTING A TOILET TANK LEVEL

If your toilet runs continuously and the water spills over into the top of the overflow tube, the first thing to try is lowering the tank level by adjusting the ball cock. If you cannot adjust the water level enough to stop the runover, the entire ball cock should be replaced. (See "Replacing a Toilet Fill Valve" on page 44.)

If the ball cock resembles Fig. A, you can adjust the water level in the tank by bending the float arm with your hands: up for a higher level, down for a lower level.

If the ball cock resembles Fig. B, the water level is adjusted by squeezing the spring clip with your fingers and sliding the float: up for a higher water level, down for a lower level.

If the ball cock resembles Fig. C, the water level is changed by turning the adjusting screw with a screwdriver: clockwise for a higher level, counter-clockwise for lower level.

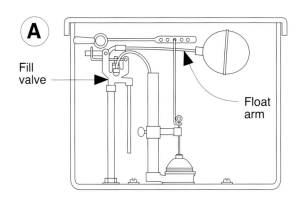

A

Fill valve

Float arm

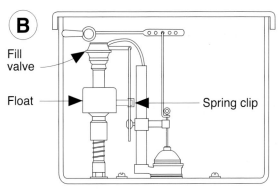

B

Fill valve

Float

Spring clip

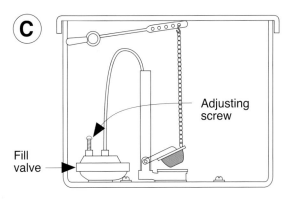

C

Adjusting screw

Fill valve

REPLACING A TOILET FILL VALVE

If your toilet runs continuously and water runs into the top of the overflow tube, lower the tank level. (See "Adjusting a Toilet Tank Level" on page 42.) If the water still runs into the overflow tube, replace the toilet fill valve—also known as the ball cock.

1. Shut off the supply valve under the tank, flush the tank and sponge the tank dry.

2. Remove the top supply coupling with an adjustable wrench.

3. Hold the ball cock with one hand and remove the locknut under the tank with the adjustable wrench (Fig. A).

4. Disconnect the bowl refill tube (Fig. B) from the overflow tube and lift the ball cock straight out.

5. Adjust the height of the new ball cock to fit in the tank by twisting its base (Fig. C).

6. Insert the threaded base of the ball cock through the hole in the bottom of the tank and secure it with the locknut.

7. Clip the bowl refill tube to the overflow tube.

8. Reconnect the supply pipe and tighten the top supply coupling with the adjustable wrench.

9. Open the supply valve under the tank and let the tank fill.

10. Flush the tank and adjust the float until the tank fills to within 2 inches of the tank rim. If the toilet doesn't flush completely, raise the float and fill level to 1 inch below the rim.

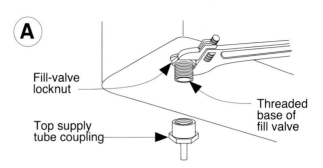

Fill-valve locknut

Threaded base of fill valve

Top supply tube coupling

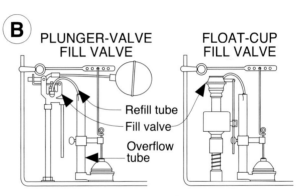

PLUNGER-VALVE FILL VALVE

FLOAT-CUP FILL VALVE

Refill tube

Fill valve

Overflow tube

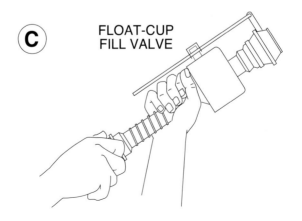

FLOAT-CUP FILL VALVE

Adjusting a Toilet Stopper

If your toilet runs continuously but the water never reaches the top of the overflow tube, the stopper may be misaligned with the flush valve seat. You can fix this problem by adjusting the stopper guide arm. If the toilet still runs after this, the stopper may be worn or cracked. (See "Replacing a Toilet Stopper" on page 48.)

1. Turn off the water supply valve under the toilet tank.

2. Flush the toilet to empty the tank and sponge the tank dry.

3. Look at the lift wire to see if it is bent. If it is, straighten it with your hands.

4. Using slip-joint pliers, loosen the guide-arm adjustment screw (Fig. B). Adjust the guide arm back and forth as necessary so that it guides the stopper directly into the flush-valve outlet. Retighten the guide-arm adjustment screw.

5. Pull up the stopper and clean the inside of the flush-valve outlet by scouring it with a scrub pad.

6. Drop the stopper into position and turn on the water-supply valve under the toilet tank.

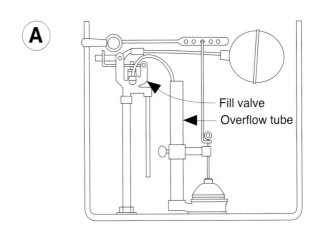

(A)

Fill valve
Overflow tube

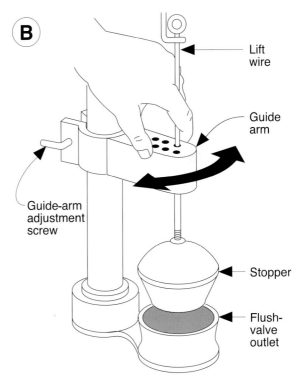

(B)

Lift wire

Guide arm

Guide-arm adjustment screw

Stopper

Flush-valve outlet

REPLACING A TOILET STOPPER

If your toilet runs continuously, but the water never reaches the top of the overflow tube, the stopper is leaking. First try adjusting the guide arm that steers the stopper into the flush hole, and clean the surface of the flush hole. If that doesn't work, replace the stopper as described below.

1. Turn off the supply valve under the toilet tank.

2. Flush the toilet to empty the tank and sponge the tank dry.

3. Unscrew the old stopper counterclockwise from the lift wire (Fig. B). If necessary, grip the top loop in the lift wire with slip-joint pliers.

4. Clean the inside of the valve seat by scouring it with a scrub pad.

5. Screw the new stopper onto the lift wire.

6. Line up the stopper with the valve seat by straightening the lift wire—if it is bent—and by adjusting the guide arm.

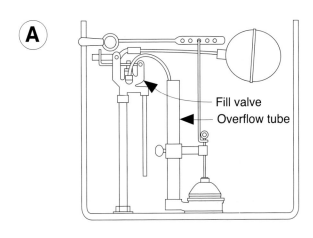

A

Fill valve
Overflow tube

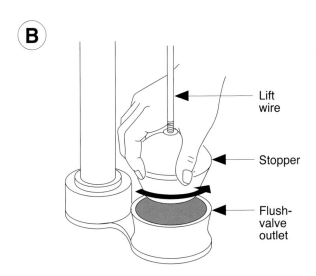

B

Lift
wire

Stopper

Flush-
valve
outlet

Cleaning Toilet-Bowl Rinse Holes

If your drinking glasses are cloudy or filmy, you probably live in an area with hard water—water containing dissolved minerals. The same lime deposits you see on glasses builds up on, and will eventually clog, the small rinse holes under the rim of a toilet bowl. Dissolving these deposits is a simple task.

1. Turn off the supply valve under the toilet tank.

2. Flush the tank to empty it. Hold the handle down to minimize the amount of water retained in the tank.

3. Roll single sheets of paper towel into tight, $1/2$-inch-diameter rolls.

4. Press the paper towel rolls up under the rim of the bowl and stick them there with plumber's putty (Fig. A).

5. Remove the tank cover, lift the stopper by the lift wire, and pour 16 ounces of commercial lime remover down the flush hole (Fig. B).

6. After 8 hours, remove the plumber's putty and paper towels, throw them in the trash, and wash your hands immediately.

7. Turn the water back on and flush the toilet.

8. If the flush holes still seem clogged, cut a 6-inch length of wire from a coat hanger with diagonal-cutting pliers and use the wire to clear the flush holes.

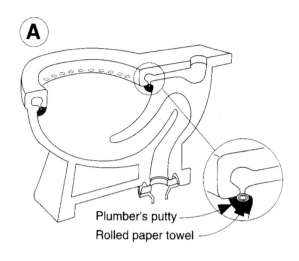

Plumber's putty
Rolled paper towel

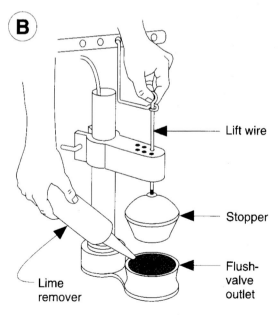

Lift wire

Stopper

Flush-
valve
outlet

Lime
remover

UNCLOGGING A TOILET

What lies beyond the flush hole in a toilet bowl is a great mystery to most homeowners. If you could see—as in the diagrams—what was blocking the flow, freeing it would be simple. Here are two common tricks. Of course the best rule is never to flush anything other than the waste the toilet is designed to handle.

1. Place the opening of a funnel-cup plunger into the drain hole at the bottom of the toilet (Fig. A).

2. Plunge up and down as hard as possible 10 times. Remove the plunger and observe the results.
3. If the toilet remains clogged, repeat Step 2.

4. If the toilet is still clogged, place the bend of a closet auger in the drain hole and feed the auger cable through the bend into the hole (Fig. B).

5. When the cable meets an obstruction—when you cannot push it any further—lock the handle with the thumbscrew and turn the handle clockwise.

6. Continuing to turn the handle clockwise, slowly withdrawing the cable. With luck, the material clogging the toilet will be hooked on the end of the cable.

7. Repeat Steps 4 through 6 until the toilet flushes normally.

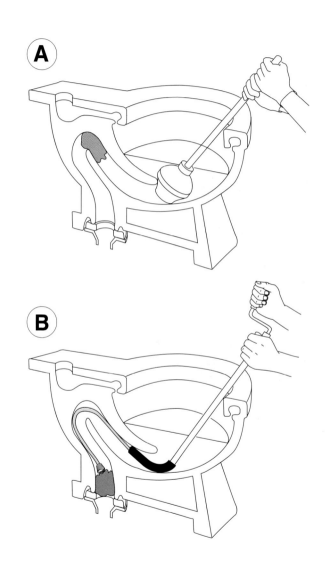

TROUBLESHOOTING TOILET LEAKS

A toilet bowl or tank with a damp exterior doesn't necessarily indicate a leak. Depending on the temperature of the water in the toilet and the temperature of the air around it, your toilet can sweat. But whether your toilet is leaking or simply sweating, the moisture can damage your floor.

1. Flush the toilet and clean it out with toilet-bowl cleaner and a toilet brush. Flush the toilet again to rinse.

2. Pour a teaspoon of food coloring into the tank and mix; let sit for one hour.

3. After the hour, wipe the base of the tank with a paper towel. If the towel shows any color, the tank is leaking. (See "Fixing a Leaking Toilet Tank" on page 58.) If the coloring doesn't show up on the towel, the moisture on the outside of the tank is caused by sweating. (See "Preventing Toilet Tank Sweating" on page 56.)

4. Flush the colored water into the bowl, and let it sit for another hour.

5. After the hour, wipe around the base of the bowl with a fresh paper towel. If it shows any color, the toilet base is leaking. (See "Fixing a Leaking Toilet Base" on page 62.) If the coloring doesn't show up on the towel, the moisture around the base is just caused by sweating. (See "Preventing Toilet Tank Sweating" on page 56.)

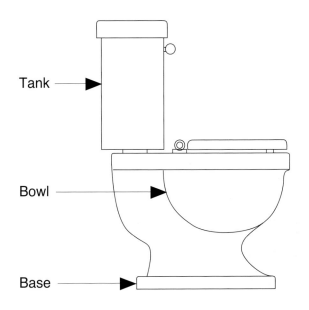

Tank

Bowl

Base

PREVENTING TOILET TANK SWEATING

Condensation often forms on the outside of toilet tanks when air humidity is high. Occasional condensation is normal; however, continuous condensation may run onto and rot the area under the toilet. Tank condensation can be prevented by insulating the inside of the tank. If someone suggests installing a valve to mix hot water into the toilet supply, agree only if they are willing to pay your hot-water bill.

1. Shut off the supply valve under the tank and flush the toilet to empty the tank.

2. Scrub the inside walls of the tank with a scrub pad, rinse, and let dry completely overnight.

3. Using a pencil, kraft paper and scissors, make patterns for the front and rear inside walls of the tank. Trim the paper to a close fit. Cut out around the tank handle.

4. Using straight pins, pin the paper patterns to $^1/_2$-inch-thick, molded polystyrene foam, and cut the foam with a utility knife. Split the front panel vertically as shown.

5. With a putty knife, apply waterproof mastic to the foam panels and press them into place.

6. Make patterns for the two side pieces, pin the patterns to foam, and cut the foam.

7. After checking the fit, make adjustments if necessary, and then apply mastic and press the side pieces into place.

8. Let the mastic dry overnight before turning the supply valve back on.

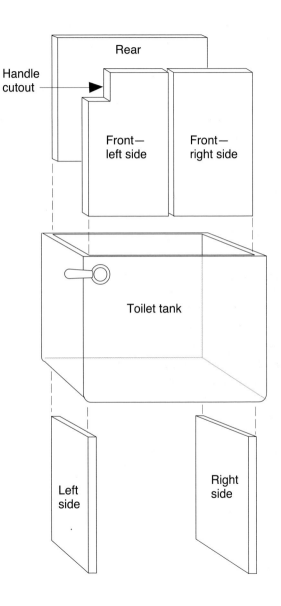

Rear

Handle cutout

Front— left side

Front— right side

Toilet tank

Left side

Right side

FIXING A LEAKING TOILET TANK

As with the suspected leaking toilet base, first pour a teaspoon of food coloring into the tank and let it sit. After an hour, wipe the bottom of the tank with a paper towel. If the towel is stained, you have a tank leak. If not, see "Preventing Toilet Tank Sweating" on page 56.

1. Determine which of the three tank connections is leaking (Fig. A):

- supply locknut—Steps 2 and 3.
- tank bolts—Steps 2 and 4.
- tank outlet—Step 2 and Steps 5 through 8.

2. Turn off the supply valve beneath the tank, flush the toilet and sponge the inside of the tank dry.

3. If the supply locknut is leaking, remove the fill valve and replace the gasket as described in "Replacing a Toilet Fill Valve" on page 44.

4. If tank bolts are leaking (Fig. B), remove the bolt with an adjustable wrench and screwdriver and replace its gasket. Do one bolt at a time to avoid disconnecting the tank.

5. If the tank outlet is leaking, remove the top supply tube coupling (Fig. B) and the two tank bolt nuts under the tank, and lift the tank straight up.

(continued on page 60)

58

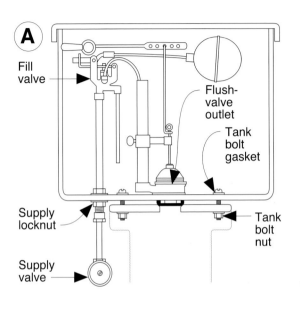

Fill valve

Flush-valve outlet

Tank bolt gasket

Supply locknut

Tank bolt nut

Supply valve

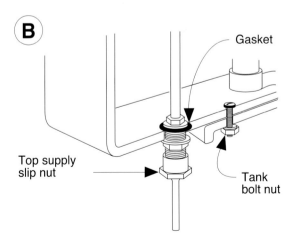

Gasket

Top supply slip nut

Tank bolt nut

6. Place a new spud washer over the flush-valve tailpiece (Fig. C).

7. Lower the tank onto the base so that the tank bolts go through the holes in the base. Attach the nuts and tighten with the adjustable wrench until just snug.

8. Reinstall the supply-tube coupling.

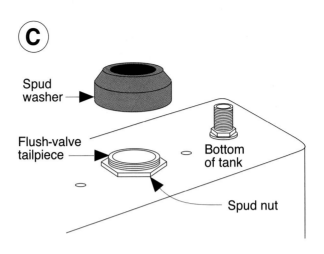

C

Spud washer

Flush-valve tailpiece

Bottom of tank

Spud nut

FIXING A LEAKING TOILET BASE

Before removing the toilet, perform a simple test to determine whether it is truly leaking or whether it is sweating. Pour a teaspoon of food coloring into the tank and let it sit for an hour. Flush the toilet and, after another hour, wipe the base with a paper towel. If the water is colored, the base is leaking. If not, see "Preventing Toilet Tank Sweating" on page 56.

1. Turn off the supply valve under the toilet tank.

2. Flush the toilet and use a sponge to remove all remaining water in the bowl and the bottom of the tank.

3. Remove the coupling nut holding the supply tube at the bottom of the tank by turning it counterclockwise with an adjustable wrench (Fig. A).

4. Pry off the closet bolt caps with a screwdriver.

5. Remove the closet bolt nuts with the adjustable wrench (Fig. B).

6. Rock the toilet back and forth slightly until it seems loose.

7. Facing the tank, straddle the toilet, lift it straight up (Fig. C) and place it on its side.

(continued on page 64)

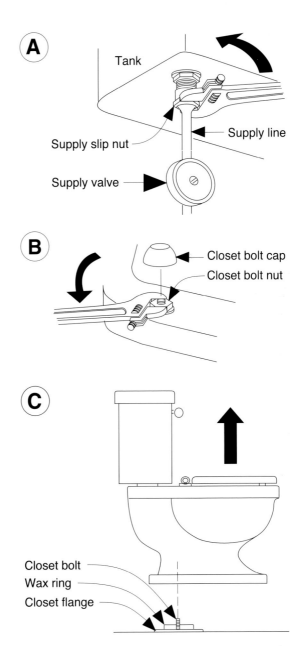

A

Tank

Supply slip nut

Supply line

Supply valve

B

Closet bolt cap

Closet bolt nut

C

Closet bolt

Wax ring

Closet flange

8. Using a putty knife, scrape the old wax from the toilet flange and the base of the toilet (Fig. D).

9. Peel the paper from a new wax toilet gasket and press the gasket over the horn of the toilet base (Fig. E).

10. Apply plumber's putty to the bottom edge of the toilet.

11. With a helper standing by, straddle the toilet again, pick it up, and hold it over the flange. Lower the toilet slowly while your helper guides the base onto the flange bolts.

12. Sit on the toilet seat to compress the plumber's putty and the wax ring.

13. Place the washers and nuts on the flange bolts and tighten the nuts with the adjustable wrench until just snug.

14. Repeat Steps 12 and 13 until the bolts no longer loosen under your weight. Do not tighten the bolts further, or you may crack the toilet base. Replace the bolt caps.

15. Reconnect the supply pipe by turning the coupling nut clockwise.

16. Turn on the water supply, fill the tank and flush the toilet. Check for leaks. Tighten the supply coupling, if necessary.

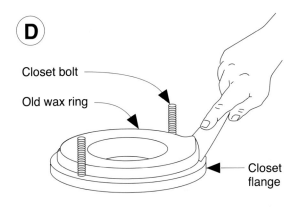

D

Closet bolt

Old wax ring

Closet flange

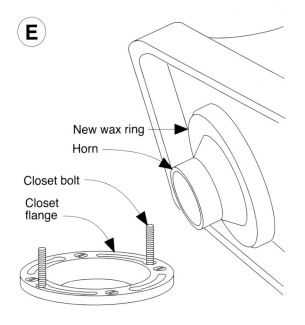

E

New wax ring

Horn

Closet bolt

Closet flange

REPLACING A TOILET SEAT

Does your toilet look old and tired? The porcelain bowl and tank can usually be cleaned up to look like new, but a chipped, stained seat should be replaced. Replacement seats can cost as little as $10; none requires more than 10 minutes to install.

1. Measure the existing toilet seat and purchase a new seat of the same overall dimensions. Except for commercial and marine versions, the great majority of toilets take the same size seats.

2. If the bolts securing the old seat are hidden under caps, pry the caps up with a screwdriver (Fig. A).

3. Hold the nut on the bottom with an adjustable wrench and turn the screw on top counterclockwise to remove the seat bolts (Fig. B). If the screw is frozen, cut it off from beneath with a hacksaw.

4. Remove the old seat and clean around the mounting holes thoroughly with a scrub pad.

5. Place the bolts of the new seat in the mounting holes, align the seat and attach the nuts. Use a screwdriver on the top and the adjustable wrench on the bottom to tighten the seat bolts firmly.

6. Snap the bolt caps—if any—closed.

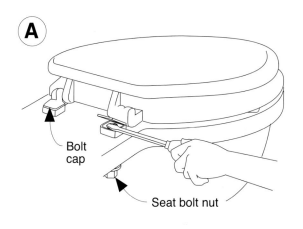

Bolt
cap

Seat bolt nut

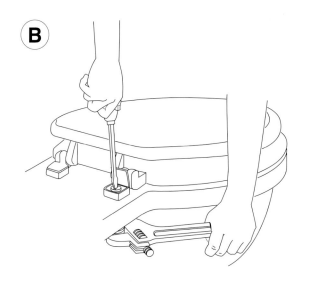

Maintaining a Septic System

If you are like most homeowners, you have no idea where the access cover to your septic tank is. If so, find out—now! If the tank totally fills up with sludge, the sludge will spill over into the drain field and clog it. Replacing the drain field can cost thousands.

1. Locate your septic tank. If you do not know where it is, call the contractor who installed it or the previous owner of your home. If all else fails, call a septic pump-out company.

2. If you haven't done so already, call a pump-out company for an inspection. Be there when they do the work.

3. Obtain the following information from the pump-out technician:

- exact location of the access cover

- depth of sludge at which the tank should be pumped.

4. Using a tape measure, sketch the distances, X and Y, of the access cover from two or more fixed locations (Fig. A). Put this sketch with your deed.

5. Make a dipstick from an 8-foot length of 1x3 strapping. Wrap the bottom 5 feet of the stick in a scrap of white sheet and staple the sheet.

6. Once per year, dig up the access cover and measure the depth of sludge—it will stick to the sheet. Hose the sludge off with a garden hose.

7. To maximize the time required between pump-outs, compost your food waste rather than feeding it to the garbage disposal.

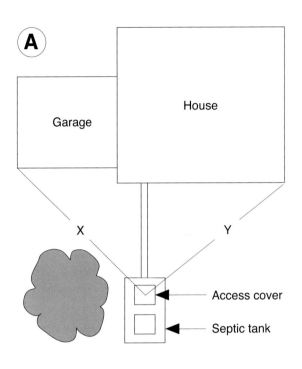

A

Garage

House

X

Y

Access cover

Septic tank

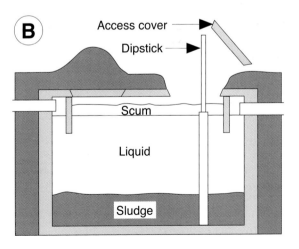

B

Access cover

Dipstick

Scum

Liquid

Sludge

ADJUSTING WATER TEMPERATURE

You may wish to adjust the temperature of your water for one of several reasons. Lowering the temperature will lower your cost of heating water. On the other hand, raising the temperature will increase the amount of heat in storage and allow longer showers. The suggested temperature of water for bathing is no more than 120°F.

1. If you have a gas water heater, adjust the thermostat on the control box (Fig. A). Change the setting by 10°F, then wait an hour before testing the water temperature at the tap with a candy thermometer.

2. If you have an electric water heater, turn off the heater circuit breaker(s) at the main panel.

3. Using a screwdriver, remove the access panel(s) and pull back the insulation to expose the thermostat(s). Unless your water heater holds less than 30 gallons, it probably has an upper and a lower heating element—each controlled by its own thermostat.

4. With the screwdriver, adjust the thermostat(s) by 10°F (Fig. B).

5. Turn the circuit breaker(s) back on and push the red reset button(s).

6. Wait an hour, then test the water temperature at the tap with a candy thermometer.

7. Repeat Steps 2, 4, 5 and 6 until the water is the right temperature.

8. Replace the insulation and the access panels.

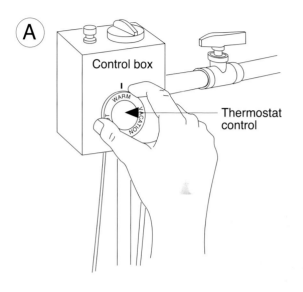

Control box

Thermostat control

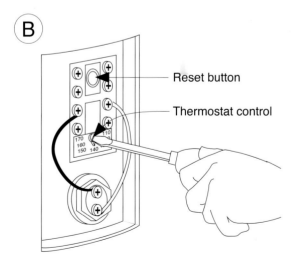

Reset button

Thermostat control

Replacing a Water-Heater Element

*If you suddenly notice you have less hot water—
and you haven't added a teenager to the household—you may have lost a heater element in your
electric water heater. Heater elements are
designed to be replaced easily, so don't panic and
ask the plumber to install a whole new tank!*

1. Determine which element—if there is more
than one—needs replacement: the top one if you
get only a small amount of hot water; the bottom
one if you get lots of water, but it is not very hot.

2. Turn off the supply valve and the circuit breaker
serving the water heater.

3. Remove the access panel (Fig. A) on the side of
the tank and pull back the insulation.

4. Connect a garden hose to the drain valve at the
bottom of the tank and empty the tank. Close the
valve and remove the hose.

5. Loosen the terminal screws of the heating element and remove the wires (Fig. B).

6. Using an adjustable wrench, remove the element
by turning it counterclockwise. Purchase a replacement element of the same volts, watts and length.

7. Coat both sides of the new gasket with pipe-
joint compound, slide the gasket over the element
and screw the element into the tank.

8. Turn on the supply, then each of the hot-water
faucets in the house until the water runs steadily.

9. Reconnect the terminals, restore the power and
press the red reset button.

10. Replace the insulation and the access panel.

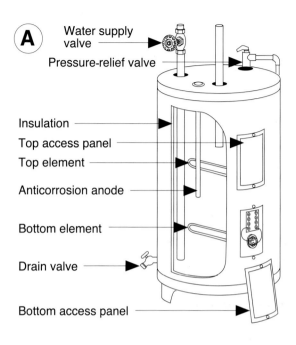

A

Water supply valve

Pressure-relief valve

Insulation

Top access panel

Top element

Anticorrosion anode

Bottom element

Drain valve

Bottom access panel

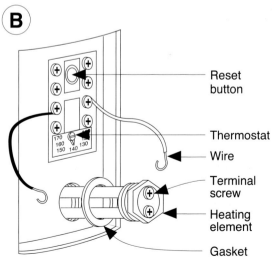

B

Reset button

Thermostat

170 160 150 140 130

Wire

Terminal screw

Heating element

Gasket

LIGHTING A GAS WATER-HEATER PILOT

If your gas supply is ever totally shut off, your pilot lights will go out and stay out until you relight them. The pilot light in a gas water heater is similar to the pilot light in a gas range.

1. With a screwdriver, remove the access panel at the bottom of the tank where the gas lines enter the tank (Fig. A).

2. Smell the opening. If you detect a strong odor of gas, call the gas company and go no further.

3. Turn the control knob on the top of the control box to "Pilot" (Fig. B).

4. Looking into the access hole with a flashlight, identify the pilot light orifice (Fig. C).

5. Light a wood match or barbecue lighter and, holding its flame to the pilot light orifice (Fig. C), press the reset button on the top of the control box. Hold the reset button down for a full minute after the pilot ignites.

6. Replace the access panel and turn the control knob to "On." The main burner should ignite. If it doesn't, turn the control knob to "Off" and call the gas company.

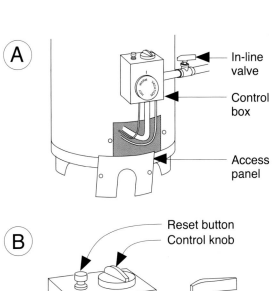

(A)

In-line valve

Control box

Access panel

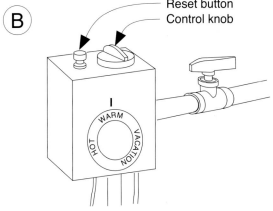

(B)

Reset button
Control knob

I

WARM

VACATION

HOT

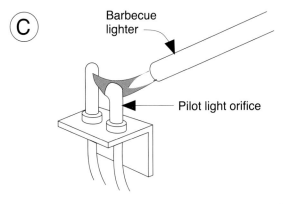

(C)

Barbecue lighter

Pilot light orifice

FIXING NOISY WATER PIPES

Water hammer is the noise a pipe makes when a water valve closes too quickly. The electric valves on clothes washers and dishwashers are the most common causes. The violent shock can be prevented either by providing an air cushion inside the pipe or a foam-rubber cushion between the pipe and the object the pipe is striking.

If the pipes bang only when the washer runs, try the following steps:

1. Turn off the clothes washer hot- and cold-water supply valves.

2. Using slip-joint pliers, remove the supply-hose couplings from the valves.

3. Screw a water hammer shock absorber onto each of the supply valves, then attach the hoses to the shock absorbers (Fig. A).

If the pipes bang even when the washer is off, try the following steps:

1. On the chance you have air chambers that have lost their air cushions, turn off the main shutoff valve—near where the water pipe enters the house— open all of your faucets until they stop running, then turn the main valve back on and turn off the faucets.

2. Have a helper turn the faucets on and off quickly to see if you still have banging and which pipes are responsible.

3. If you find a pipe that is banging into a joist or stud, cut a short length of foam pipe insulation with a utility knife and slip it over the pipe at the impact point to cushion the hammering (Fig. B).

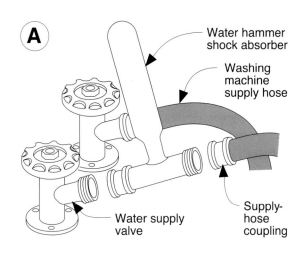

A

Water hammer shock absorber

Washing machine supply hose

Water supply valve

Supply-hose coupling

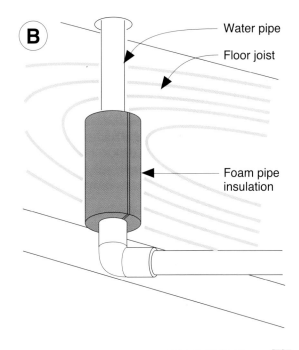

B

Water pipe

Floor joist

Foam pipe insulation

DEFROSTING A FROZEN PIPE

Many homeowners in the northern-most states have experienced frozen pipes. The key to successful recovery is melting the frozen water, but not turning it into explosive steam. Work from an open faucet toward the frozen section, and never let the pipe get too hot to touch.

1. Shut off the main water supply (Fig. A).

2. Locate the section of frozen pipe.

3. Open the valve nearest the frozen section so that any steam you accidentally generate will have an exit and not burst the pipe.

4. Starting at the open valve, heat the pipe with a hair dryer (Fig. B). Hold the nozzle 6 inches from the pipe and move it back and forth as if you were spray painting. It is all right to use high heat as long as the pipe remains cool enough to touch. Advance along the pipe at about 1 foot per minute.

5. If you do not have a hair dryer, wrap a bath towel around the pipe and pour hot water over the towel (Fig. C). As soon as the towel cools to room temperature, slide it several feet and repeat with more hot water.

6. If it looks like pipe-freezing weather again, let a faucet on this pipeline dribble. Moving water does not freeze.

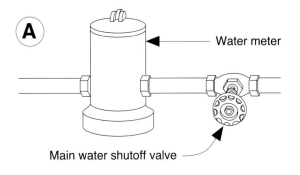

A — Water meter

Main water shutoff valve

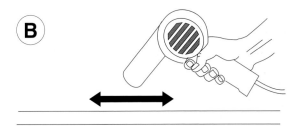

B

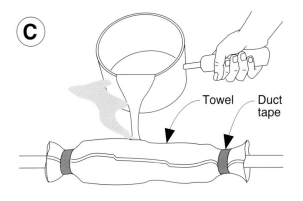

C

Towel   Duct tape

PATCHING A LEAKING PIPE

The ultimate cure for a leaking pipe is replacement. If replacement is inconvenient at the time, leaks can be patched as if they were bicycle tubes. A good temporary patch may actually last years.

1. Determine whether the leak is through a split or through a pinhole (Fig. A). Splits are due to the expansion of freezing water. Pinholes are due to corrosion inside the pipe.

2. Measure the outside diameter of the pipe. If you don't have a caliper, measure the circumference with a tape measure and divide by 3.

3. Purchase a sheet of $^1/_{16}$-inch-thick neoprene rubber or a bicycle-tube patch, plus either a sleeve clamp or a hose clamp the same diameter as the pipe.

4. If the split or hole has a rough edge, file it smooth with a flat file.

5. Using scissors, cut a rubber patch about 1 inch square for a pinhole, or 1 inch wide and 1 inch longer than a split.

6. Center the patch over the hole and install the clamp (Fig. B). Tighten the clamp as tightly as you can.

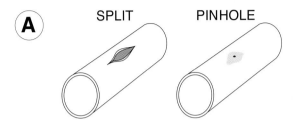

SPLIT   PINHOLE

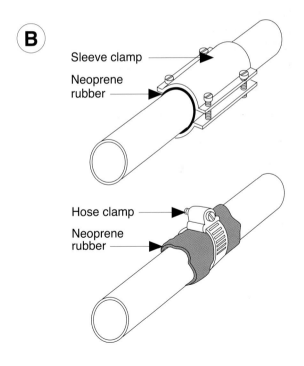

Sleeve clamp

Neoprene
rubber

Hose clamp

Neoprene
rubber

WIRING

REPLACING A SINGLE-POLE SWITCH

Since they contain moving parts, switches are subject to wear. Fortunately, they cost little and are easy to replace. Note the difference between single-pole and three-way switches, however. They are not interchangeable.

1. Turn off the power to the switch circuit at the main panel.

2. Remove the switch cover plate.

3. Remove the two screws fastening the switch to the box.

4. Holding the switch by the fastening tabs at top and bottom, pull it straight out of the box, being careful not to touch the screws to the box (Fig. A).

5. Touch one probe of a neon circuit tester to each of the terminals on the side of the switch (Fig. B). If the tester glows, you have not shut off the power.

6. Inspect the switch. If there are three wires, it is a three-way switch. (See "Replacing a Three-Way Switch" on page 86.)

7. Remove the switch by loosening its terminals and removing the wires.

8. Purchase a replacement switch of the same type. If your house wiring is aluminum—silver color—make sure the switch is marked CO/ALR, indicating compatibility with both copper and aluminum wiring.

9. Refasten the wires to the terminals on the new switch. The order makes no difference, but make sure that the word OFF faces up on the switch.

10. Fold the wires back into the box, refasten the receptacle and restore power.

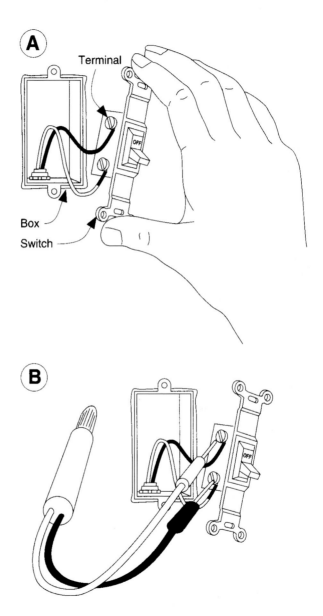

A

Terminal

Box

Switch

B

REPLACING A THREE-WAY SWITCH

A pair of three-way switches allows you to control a light from two different locations. The three-way switch has three terminals instead of the usual two, but replacement is no more difficult. But before you replace the switch, try a new bulb.

1. Turn off the power to the switch circuit at the main panel.

2. Remove the cover plate and the two screws fastening the switch to the box.

3. Holding the switch by the fastening tabs at top and bottom, pull it straight out of the box, being careful not to touch the terminals to the box (Fig. A).

4. Touch one probe of a neon circuit tester to each of the screw terminals on the side of the switch (Fig. B). If the tester glows, you have not shut off the power; try again.

5. With masking tape, label the wire under the darkest of the three terminal screws COM (Fig. C).

6. Remove the switch by loosening the terminals and removing the wires.

7. Purchase a replacement three-way switch. If your house wiring is aluminum—silver color—make sure the switch is marked CO/ALR, indicating compatibility with both copper and aluminum wiring.

8. Refasten the wires to the terminals on the new switch, making sure the wire labeled COM goes to the darkest screw.

9. Refasten the receptacle and restore power. If the light doesn't come on, you've probably replaced the wrong switch of the three-way pair. Replace the other switch with the one you just removed.

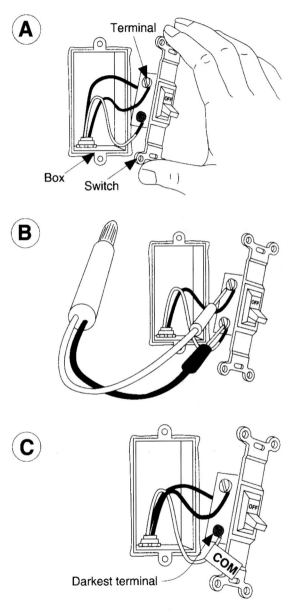

(A) Terminal

Box

Switch

(B)

(C)

Darkest terminal — COM

INSTALLING A DIMMER SWITCH

Are you tired of burning and buying candles? As expensive as electricity may be, electric light is far less expensive than candlelight. A dimmer switch can produce nearly any degree of warmth you wish. Most dimmer switches don't work with fluorescent lights, however.

1. Turn the power off at the main panel.

2. Remove the switch cover plate, loosen the switch screws, and pull the switch straight out (Fig. A).

3. Determine the type of switch: a single-pole—the most common—has two screws; the three-way—controlled from two locations—has three screws. If there are three screws, mark the wire under the darkest screw with a piece of masking tape.

4. Purchase the same type—single-pole or three-way—dimmer switch.

5. Straighten the ends of the feed wires with long-nose pliers.

6. Connect each of the dimmer wires to the feed wires by placing the tips of matching wires together and screwing on wire nuts (Fig. B). If there are three wires, the red dimmer wire connects to the wire you marked in Step 4.

7. Test the connections by tugging on the wires to be sure they are tight, then fold the wires back into the box, allowing room for the switch.

8. Screw the new switch to the box.

9. Replace the cover plate, restore power and test your new dimmer.

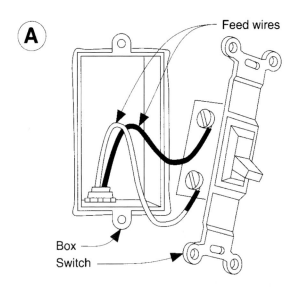

Feed wires

Box

Switch

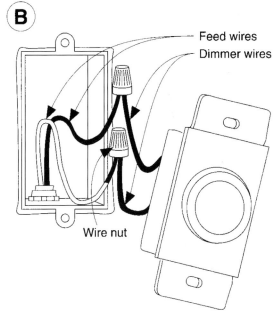

Feed wires

Dimmer wires

Wire nut

REPLACING A TWO-PRONG PLUG

Replacing a two-prong plug is simple since the invention of the quick-connect replacement plug. The only reason you need a wire stripper is to cut the cord to the desired length. A sturdy pair of sewing shears will serve as well. Note the difference between polarized and nonpolarized plugs. Do not substitute one for the other.

1. Cut off the old plug with diagonal-cutting pliers.

2. Take the old plug to the store and purchase a quick-connect replacement plug with the same prong pattern (Fig. A):

> • The prongs of a nonpolarized plug are of the same width.

> • The prongs of a polarized plug are of different widths.

3. Separate the prong assembly of the new plug from its casing by squeezing the prongs together and pulling the casing off.

4. Without removing any insulation, insert the old cord through the casing.

5. Spread the prongs and push the cord into the prong assembly all the way (Fig. B). Important: If the plug is polarized, orient the cord so that the side with the groove goes into the side with the wider prong.

6. Squeeze the two prongs together (Fig. C).

7. Push the closed prong assembly into the plug casing (Fig. D).

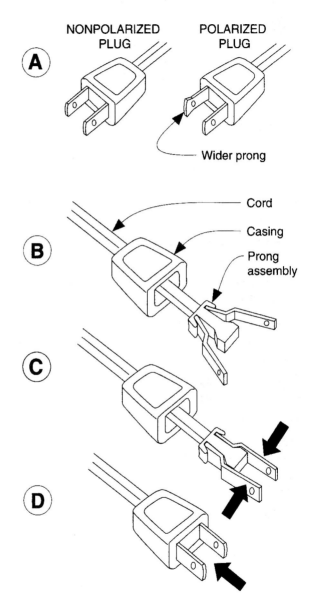

NONPOLARIZED
PLUG

POLARIZED
PLUG

Wider prong

Cord

Casing

Prong
assembly

REPLACING A THREE-PRONG PLUG

Three-prong plugs are not available in quick-connect versions, but they are still easy to replace. The most difficult part of replacing one is tying the Underwriters' knot. If that looks too difficult, purchase a three-prong plug with a screw clamp for gripping the cord.

1. Cut off the old plug with diagonal-cutting pliers, take it to the store and purchase a replacement rated at the same amps and volts (Fig. A).

2. Remove the insulated disk of the new plug, exposing the inside.

3. Insert the cord through the rear of the new plug.

4. Split the cord sheathing back $2^1/_2$ inches with a utility knife and remove.

5. Strip $^1/_2$ inch of insulation from each of the conductors with a wire stripper.

6. If there is room inside the plug, tie the black and white wires into an Underwriters' knot to eliminate strain on the terminals (Fig. B). Pull on the cord until the knot bottoms in the plug.

7. Twist the end of each wire to pull the wire strands together. Then secure each wire under its screw by looping the end clockwise around the screw and tightening the screw (Fig. C). Place the white wire under the silver screw, the black wire under the brass screw, and the green wire under the green or darkest screw.

8. Make sure no errant strands of wire are touching the adjacent screw.

9. Replace the insulated disk.

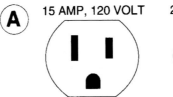
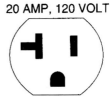

(A) 15 AMP, 120 VOLT   20 AMP, 120 VOLT

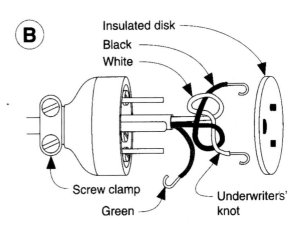

(B)

Insulated disk

Black

White

Screw clamp

Green

Underwriters' knot

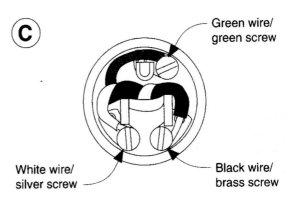

(C)

Green wire/ green screw

White wire/ silver screw

Black wire/ brass screw

TESTING A RECEPTACLE

Too few homeowners and apartment dwellers know about the $5 receptacle tester and the equally low-cost neon circuit tester. It's a good idea to test every receptacle in and around your home to anticipate problems before they zap you. Improperly connected receptacles can shock you, damage electronic equipment and cause fires.

Three-slot receptacle: plug in a receptacle tester, available at hardware stores for about $5 (Fig. A). Match the pattern of lights against the patterns shown on the tester label. (Fig. B shows a typical label.)

Two-slot receptacle: use a neon circuit tester (Fig. C). Holding the probes of the tester by their insulated sleeves, touch them to the long slot (L), the short slot (S), and the grounding screw (G) in the following order:

- L and S—The tester should glow. If not, there is no power to the circuit.

- S and G—If the tester glows, the receptacle box is grounded, and you can install a more modern three-slot receptacle. If not, go to the next test.

- L and G—If the tester glows, the black and white wires to the receptacle are reversed. If not, the receptacle box is not grounded, and you should not use a two-to-three prong adapter, nor should you install a three-slot receptacle.

To rectify a problem, compare the miswired receptacle to one that is properly wired, and reroute the wiring as if you were replacing the receptacle. (See "Replacing a Receptacle" on page 96.)

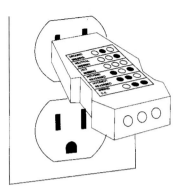

B) TYPICAL TROUBLESHOOTING GUIDE
(Black is Illuminated light)

○●○	**GROUND MISSING**	Ground (bare or green) wire missing or disconnected
○○●	**NEUTRAL MISSING**	Neutral (white) wire missing or disconnected
○○○	**HOT MISSING**	Hot (black) wire missing or disconnected
●○●	**HOT/GND REVERSED**	Hot (black) and ground (bare or green) wires reversed
●●○	**HOT/NEUT REVERSED**	Hot (black) and neutral (white) wires reversed
○●●	**WIRING O.K.**	All wires properly connected

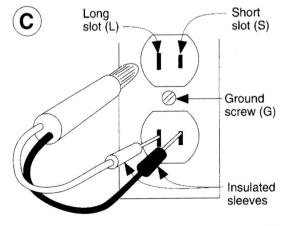

Long slot (L)

Short slot (S)

Ground screw (G)

Insulated sleeves

REPLACING A RECEPTACLE

Receptacles do wear out and break. If one of yours is giving you trouble, first try bending or spreading the prongs of the plug that you're plugging into the receptacle. This will help the receptacle make a stronger contact. If the receptacle still doesn't work, replace it; new ones cost less than a fast-food quarter-pounder.

1. Check your receptacle with Fig. A to determine if you have a ground or polarized receptacle.

2. Turn off power at the main panel.

3. Remove the receptacle cover plate, remove the screws securing the receptacle to the box and pull the receptacle out.

4. Touch the probes of a neon circuit tester to the upper silver and brass screws on the sides. Repeat with the lower set of screws. If the tester glows, you did not turn off the correct circuit; try again.

5. Before removing any wires, label each with masking tape: S for silver, B for brass and G for green (Fig. B).

6. Loosen the terminal screws and remove the wires.

7. Purchase an identical receptacle. Do not replace a two-prong with a three-prong receptacle. If any tabs are missing on the original unit, remove them on the replacement receptacle as well, to separate the two outlets electrically.

8. Reconnect the labeled wires.

9. Fold the wires back into the box, refasten the receptacle to the box and restore the power.

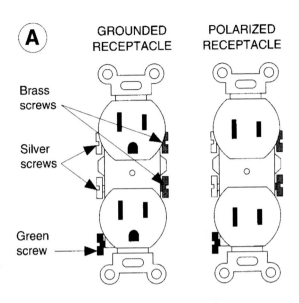

A GROUNDED RECEPTACLE   POLARIZED RECEPTACLE

Brass screws

Silver screws

Green screw

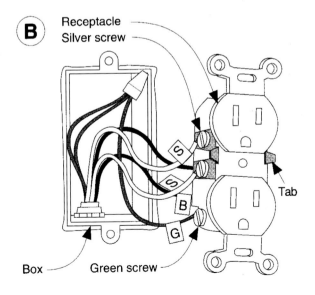

B Receptacle
Silver screw

S

S

B

G

Tab

Box — Green screw

INSTALLING A GFCI

A ground-fault circuit interrupter (GFCI) has a built-in circuit breaker that protects you against lethal shocks by shutting down a circuit or receptacle when it detects a problem. You should install GFCI receptacles in bathrooms, kitchens and outdoors.

1. Turn off the power to the circuit at the main panel.

2. If there is more than one receptacle to test, test each receptacle—they may be on different circuits—by inserting the probes of a neon circuit tester into the two rectangular slots of each outlet. If the bulb glows, you haven't found both circuits; try again.

3. Remove the receptacle cover plate.

4. Remove the receptacle screws, and pull the receptacle straight out (Fig. A).

5. Disconnect all wires from the receptacle. The black and white wires may be held by screws on the side, or they may be inserted into holes in the back of the receptacle. Inserted wires may be released by inserting the blade of a narrow screwdriver or a thin nail into the slots adjacent to the wires and pulling the wires out (Fig. B).

6. Cut off a 4-inch length of 12-2 NM with ground cable with diagonal-cutting pliers. Pull the insulated wires out of the sheathing, and strip $^3/_4$ inch of insulation from both ends of each wire with a wire stripper.

(continued on page 100)

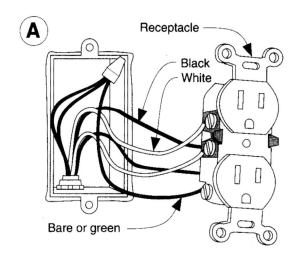

(A) Receptacle

Black
White

Bare or green

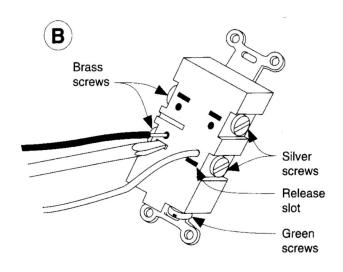

(B) Brass screws

Silver screws

Release slot

Green screws

7. With long-nose pliers, make a circle of one end of the black wire, insert it under the GFCI terminal labeled LINE-BLACK, and tighten the screw clockwise (Fig. C).

8. Fasten one end of the white wire to the GFCI terminal labeled LINE-WHITE in the same manner.

9. Fasten the one end of the bare wire under the GFCI green screw.

10. Connect the loose ends of all of the white wires by holding their ends together, inserting the wires into a wire nut, and twisting the wire nut clockwise until tight. Check the connection by pulling on each of the wires (Fig. D).

11. Repeat Step 10 with all of the black wires and again with all of the bare wires.

12. Carefully fold all of the wires back into the box. Then insert and secure the GFCI, making sure none of the bare wires are contacting any of the screw terminals at the sides of the GFCI. If the box is too small to hold the wires and the receptacle, purchase a box extension at a home center.

13. Install the special GFCI cover plate.

14. Restore power and test the GFCI by pushing on the button labeled TEST. The GFCI breaker should click and turn off the power to the outlet.

15. Restore power to the GFCI by pushing on the button labeled RESET.

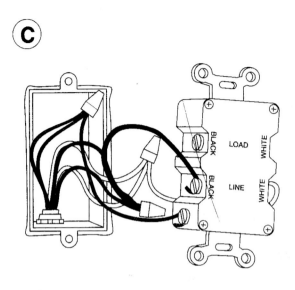

BLACK LOAD WHITE

BLACK LINE WHITE

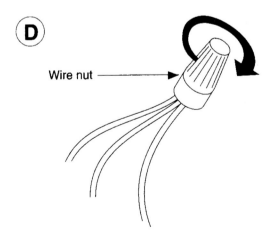

Wire nut

REPLACING A SWITCHED RECEPTACLE

A switched receptacle is used for controlling table and floor lamps from a wall switch. If you label the wires as suggested, you will have no problem replacing the receptacle. Test the receptacle before replacing it. (See "Testing a Receptacle" on page 94.)

1. Turn off the power to the receptacle circuit at the main panel.

2. Remove the cover plate and the two screws fastening the switch to the box.

3. Holding the receptacle by the fastening tabs at top and bottom, pull it straight out of the box, being careful not to touch the terminals to the box (Fig. A).

4. Touch one probe of a neon circuit tester to the green screw and the other probe to each of the screw terminals on the sides of the receptacle. If the tester glows, you have not shut off the power.

5. Before removing any of the wires, label each with masking tape (Fig. B).

6. Unscrew the terminals and remove the wires. Purchase a receptacle of the same volt and amp ratings. If your wiring is aluminum, make sure the receptacle is marked CO/ALR, indicating compatibility with both copper and aluminum wiring.

7. Refasten the wires to the new receptacle, using the labels as your guide. If any of the side tabs between the screw terminals of the old receptacle were broken off to separate the two outlets electrically, break them off the new receptacle as well, using long-nose pliers.

8. Fold the wires back into the box, refasten the receptacle and restore power.

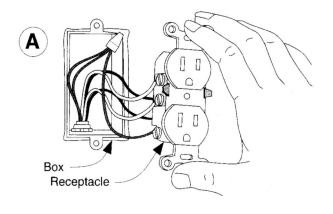

Box

Receptacle

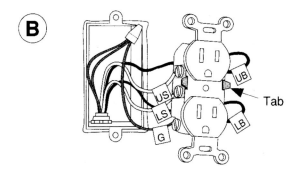

Tab

INSTALLING A GROUNDED RECEPTACLE

Many older homes have two-slot receptacles. If the metal box housing is grounded, a two-slot receptacle can be converted to a three-slot receptacle. To determine whether yours can be converted, perform the tests in "Testing a Receptacle" on page 94.

1. Turn off the power at the main panel. Test the receptacle with a neon circuit tester to make sure the power is off.

2. Remove the receptacle cover plate, remove the screws securing the receptacle to the box, and pull the receptacle out.

3. Label each wire with masking tape: S for silver and B for brass, then loosen the terminal screws and remove the wires.

4. Replace the two-prong with a three-prong receptacle. If any tabs are missing on the original unit, remove them on the replacement receptacle as well to separate the two outlets electrically.

5. Reconnect the labeled wires.

6. Fasten a grounding pigtail under a screw at the back of the box and a second pigtail under the green screw on the receptacle, then twist the two pigtails together with a wire nut.

7. Fold the wires back into the box, refasten the receptacle to the box, and restore the power.

8. For a temporary conversion, plug in a grounding adapter plug and fasten the spade lug of its green grounding wire under the cover-plate screw. Before using, test the adapter plug with a receptacle tester. (See "Testing a Receptacle" on page 94.)

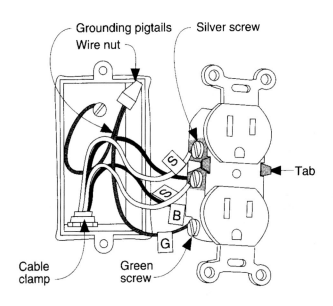

Grounding pigtails
Wire nut
Silver screw
Tab
Cable clamp
Green screw

HEATING AND
COOLING

BLEEDING BASEBOARDS AND RADIATORS

If you are getting heat from some baseboards or radiators, but not from others, the cool ones may have air locks. Air in the vertical loop is buoyant and prevents heated water from flowing up into the unit. The cure is to remove the air through the bleeder valve.

1. Turn the heating system on and wait until at least one baseboard convector (Fig. A) or radiator (Fig. B) gets warm. If your home has more than one thermostat, make sure all are set high enough to call for heat.

2. Check each radiator or baseboard in the house. Note any units that remain cold. Also note any units that make gurgling or banging sounds. Note, though, that it is normal for them to creak and click as they warm.

3. On each of the problem units, turn the inlet valve—handle, knob or screw—fully counterclockwise to make sure the unit is open to flow.

4. Hold a cup next to the bleeder screw and turn the screw counterclockwise until a steady stream of water flows out. Close the screw by turning it fully clockwise.

5. If after 10 minutes the unit is still cold, call your heating contractor.

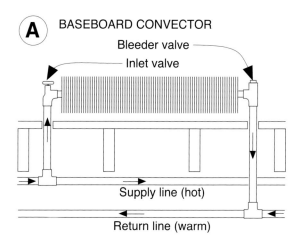

A BASEBOARD CONVECTOR

Bleeder valve

Inlet valve

Supply line (hot)

Return line (warm)

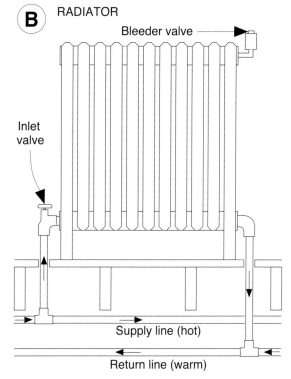

B RADIATOR

Bleeder valve

Inlet valve

Supply line (hot)

Return line (warm)

REPLACING A FURNACE FUEL FILTER

An oil heating system usually has a fuel filter between the fuel storage tank and the burner to trap impurities before they clog the extremely small opening in the oil burner nozzle. The filter should be replaced every heating season before it becomes completely clogged and cuts off the fuel supply.

1. Turn off the red emergency switch.

2. Locate the fuel filter between the fuel tank and the burner (Fig. A).

3. Close the shutoff valve (Fig. B) by turning it clockwise. If the handle is a lever, turn it perpendicular to the fuel line.

4. Place a large cake pan under the filter and, holding the body in one hand, turn the top bolt counterclockwise with an adjustable wrench.

5. When the body drops, remove the cartridge and rubber gasket and place both in the pan (Fig. C).

6. Empty the body and wipe the inside clean with a paper towel.

7. Empty the cartridge and take it to an auto-parts store to find a replacement.

8. Smear the new gasket with fuel and insert it into the groove in the body.

9. Place the new cartridge in the body, seat the body under the cap and tighten the bolt clockwise.

10. Turn on the fuel valve and then, after 5 minutes, the emergency switch and thermostat.

11. Check the filter for leaks. Tighten the bolt as necessary to stop any leak.

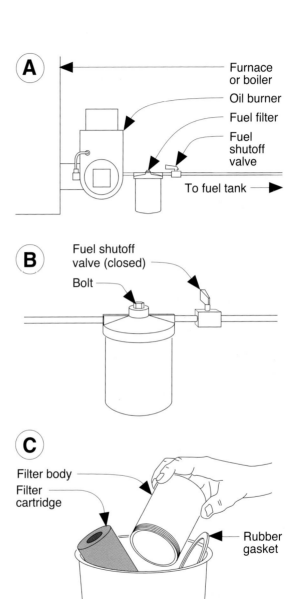

A
Furnace or boiler
Oil burner
Fuel filter
Fuel shutoff valve
To fuel tank →

B
Fuel shutoff valve (closed)
Bolt

C
Filter body
Filter cartridge
Rubber gasket

BALANCING FORCED-AIR HEAT

Some rooms have higher heat loss than other rooms, so you need a way to proportion the airflow among rooms. Among the rooms controlled by a single thermostat, that control is provided by dampers in the ducts. By closing a damper, you reduce the rate of flow through its duct.

1. To maximize the efficiency of the heating system, you want airflow as free as possible, so begin by opening all floor and wall registers fully. Also make sure than none of the registers is covered by rugs or other furnishings.

2. In the basement, trace all of the ducts leading from the supply plenum (Fig. A), looking for damper handles. Turn all damper handles parallel to the direction of the ducts (Fig. B).

3. On a cold night—not a sunny day, because of solar heating effects—adjust the thermostat until the coldest room is at the desired temperature.

4. Partially close the supply registers, if adjustable, or locate and partially close the dampers in the supply ducts to the rooms that are too warm.

5. Wait an hour for the temperatures to stabilize. If the too-warm rooms are still too warm, close the registers or dampers a bit more. If too cool, partially open the registers or dampers. Continue waiting and adjusting until all rooms are at the desired temperature.

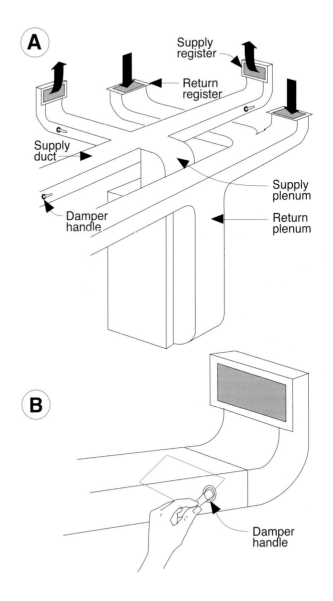

A

Supply register

Return register

Supply duct

Supply plenum

Return plenum

Damper handle

B

Damper handle

REPLACING A FORCED-AIR FILTER

Warm-air heating systems contain large fibrous filters in the ducts that return air to the furnace. The filter removes airborne dust before it can be deposited inside the furnace and supply ducts or on household surfaces. A dirty filter makes the furnace work harder, so replace the filter several times during each heating season.

1. On the furnace, identify the return plenum (Fig. A). If you have trouble locating it, turn up the thermostat until the furnace comes on. After 5 minutes, feel the ducts connected to the furnace. The supply plenum and all of the ducts leading from it will be warm; the return plenum and ducts feeding into it will be cool.

2. Turn the furnace off and let it cool. Turn off the red emergency furnace switch—usually located at the entrance to the basement or furnace room.

3. Locate and remove the furnace filter (Fig. B). It will be located either in a slot in the side of the return plenum or inside the furnace blower compartment, accessed by a panel or door.

4. If the filter is washable—not cardboard—spray it forcefully with a garden hose to clean it. Otherwise, take the old filter to the hardware store or home center and purchase half a dozen replacement filters of the same type and size.

5. Install a new filter and restore power to the furnace.

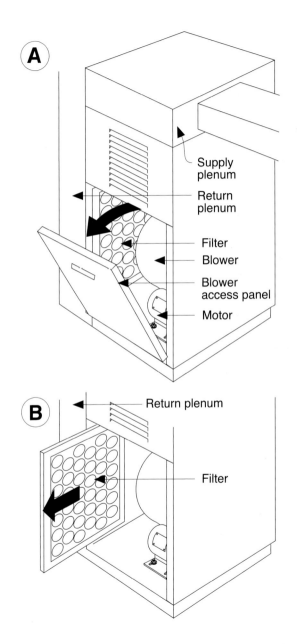

A

Supply plenum

Return plenum

Filter

Blower

Blower access panel

Motor

B

Return plenum

Filter

Relighting a Gas Furnace Pilot

A gas furnace pilot may go out because of a sudden gust of wind or because the gas was temporarily cut off. A thermocouple near the pilot flame senses when the pilot is off and shuts off the gas supply before an explosive situation develops. The pilot is easy to relight, but first read the instructions specific to your equipment.

1. Read the instructions on the front or side of the furnace to see if they differ from those below.

2. Turn off the gas inlet valve and the manual control knob (Fig. A). Allow 30 minutes for any accumulated gas to dissipate. If you still smell gas after 30 minutes, call the gas company.

3. Turn the room thermostat to "Off."

4. Turn the manual control knob to "Pilot" and light the pilot with either a gas grill lighter (Fig. B) or a long wooden match. Hold the manual control knob in the "Pilot" position for a full minute before releasing it.

5. Turn the manual control knob to the "On" position.

6. If the pilot now goes out, call the gas company and don't go any further.

7. If the pilot stays on, turn the room thermostat to a high setting and verify that the main burner comes on. If not, call the gas company.

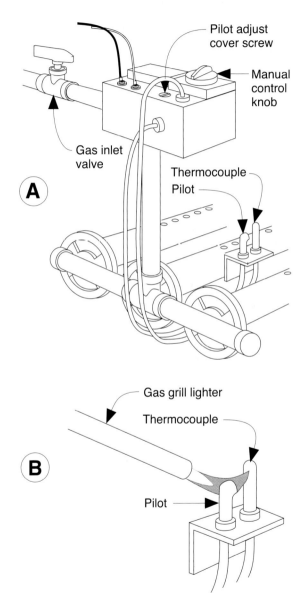

Pilot adjust
cover screw

Manual
control
knob

Gas inlet
valve

Thermocouple
Pilot

A

Gas grill lighter

Thermocouple

Pilot

B

HEATING AND COOLING **117**

CLEANING CENTRAL AC COILS

The coil that dissipates the heat from your house resembles a car radiator. To remove the heat, air is drawn through the honeycomb-like fins of the coil. The smallest deposit of dirt on the fins reduces the efficiency of the air conditioner and increases your cooling bill. Clean the coils annually.

1. Turn off the power to the outdoor air-conditioning unit and remove the cover (Fig. A).

2. Loosen the dirt on the outside face of the condenser coil using a toothbrush or other stiff, non-metallic brush. Take care not to bend the fins.

3. Either vacuum up or blow away the loosened dirt from the coil (Fig. B).

4. Cover all of the air conditioner, except the condenser coil, with a drop cloth or large plastic bag to protect the electrical components.

5. Spray the condenser coil from the inside of the unit toward the outside, using a garden hose and maximum water pressure (Fig. C).

6. Remove the drop cloth or plastic bag and replace the cover.

7. Restore the electricity.

118

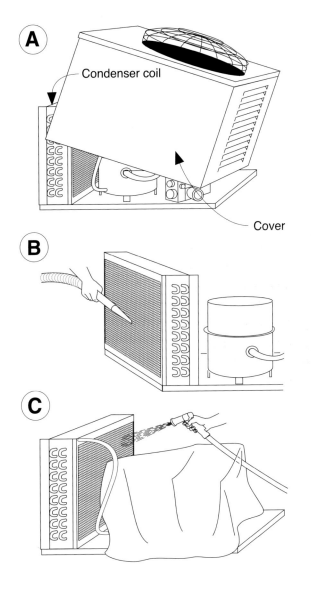

A — Condenser coil / Cover

B

C

CLEANING WINDOW AC COILS

The coil that dissipates the heat from an air conditioner resembles a car radiator. To remove the heat, air is drawn through the honeycomb-like fins of the coil. A small deposit of dirt on the fins reduces its efficiency and increases your cooling bill. Clean the coils annually.

1. Unplug the air conditioner and remove the snap-on front panel (Fig. A).

2. Before removing the air-conditioner unit from its exterior metal housing, have a table or other horizontal surface on which to place the unit. Warning: The unit will weigh at least 50 pounds.

3. Remove the screws or other fasteners that secure the unit inside its exterior metal housing.

4. Slide the unit forward into the room from the housing. If the unit suddenly resists, look for a green grounding wire attached to the housing. If there is one, unscrew it. Replace the screw so that it will not be misplaced.

5. Place the unit on the table or other horizontal surface (Fig. B).

6. Use a toothbrush to loosen the dirt from the outdoor side of the coil. Vacuum to remove the dirt (Fig. C).

7. Slide the unit back into its exterior metal housing, reattach the green grounding wire if there is one and replace the front panel and power plug.

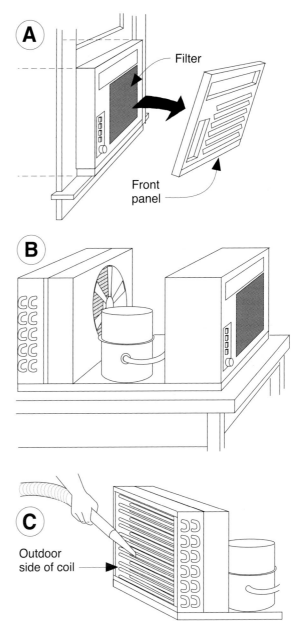

Filter

Front
panel

Outdoor
side of coil

Cleaning a Window AC Filter

Behind the front panel of a window air conditioner is a fibrous filter intended to prevent dust from entering your home. The more efficient the filter, the more often it needs cleaning. If your air conditioner is not working as well as it used to, it may be because the filter needs cleaning.

1. Remove the snap-on front panel (Fig. A).

2. Pull out the flexible filter (Fig. B). If it is torn, buy a replacement at the hardware store. If it is still intact, you can wash it.

3. Take the filter outdoors, and place it face down on a deck, driveway or other clean surface.

4. Spray the filter with maximum water pressure from a garden hose until no more dirt comes out (Fig. C).

5. Slap the filter on the deck or driveway repeatedly to shake out the moisture, and let the filter dry in the sun.

6. Replace the filter and the front panel on the air conditioner.

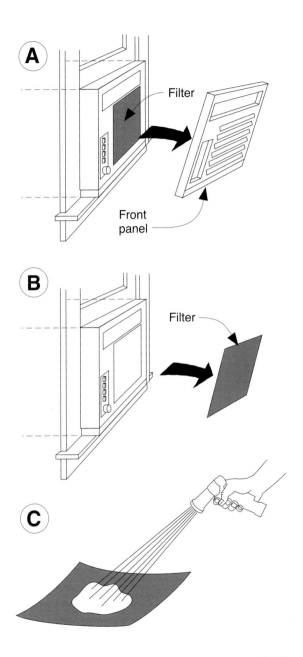

A

Filter

Front
panel

B

Filter

C

LIGHTING

REPLACING A LAMP CORD

Lamp cords suffer from being walked on by adults and chewed by children and dogs. Although it is possible to splice a lamp cord, it is as simple and far safer to replace the entire cord. This technique can also be used in making your own lamp.

1. Unplug the lamp.

2. Remove the light bulb(s).

3. Disassemble the lamp as shown in the figure.

4. Loosen the terminals and remove wire ends.

5. If threading the new wire through the lamp base appears difficult, cut the plug from the old cord with diagonal-cutting pliers and tape the end of the new cord to the cut end of the old cord with electrical tape.

6. Pull the old cord up through the base until the new cord appears.

7. Separate the two wires of the new cord back 2 inches with a utility knife.

8. Trim each wire back $^3/_4$ inch with a wire stripper.

9. Tie the Underwriters' knot shown in the illustration.

10. Twist the end of each wire. Then secure each wire by looping the end clockwise around its terminal screw and tighten the screw.

11. Reassemble the lamp.

12. If you also need a new plug, see "Replacing a Two-Prong Plug" on page 90.

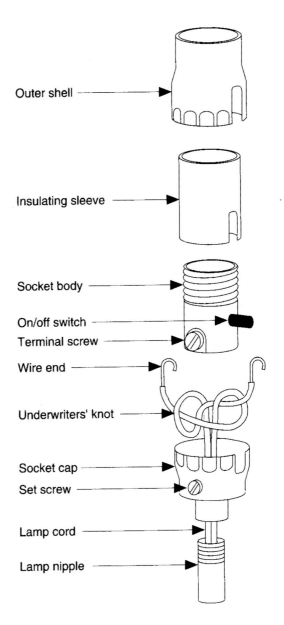

Outer shell

Insulating sleeve

Socket body

On/off switch

Terminal screw

Wire end

Underwriters' knot

Socket cap

Set screw

Lamp cord

Lamp nipple

REPAIRING A LAMP

If you have a balky lamp, don't fret. It's usually easy to fix, and the electrical components are very standardized. Hardware stores and home centers generally carry all of the common parts. If you have trouble finding a part, consult an antique dealer—they have sources.

1. First, check the lamp by switching receptacles and by replacing the bulb.

2. If it still doesn't work, unplug the lamp and disassemble it from the top down (Fig. A).

3. Unscrew the top nut and remove the shade.

4. Squeeze the socket shell at its base and work it up and off.

5. Remove the insulating sleeve.

6. Plug the lamp in and carefully touch the probes of a neon circuit tester to the two exposed terminal screws, making sure not to touch the tips against any metal. If the neon bulb lights, go to Step 7. If not, see "Replacing a Lamp Cord" on page 126.

7. Unplug the lamp again, and remove the two terminal screws and wires.

8. Take the old socket body to the store and purchase a replacement.

9. Install the socket body by looping the ends of the lamp cord wires under the terminal screws of the new socket body and tightening the screws (Fig. B).

10. Slide the insulating sleeve over the socket and press the socket shell down until it snaps into place.

11. Screw in the bulb, plug in the lamp and switch the lamp on to test.

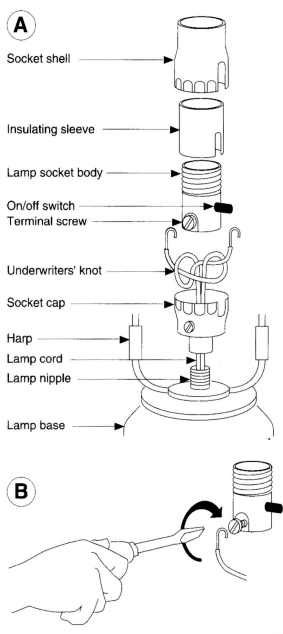

A

Socket shell

Insulating sleeve

Lamp socket body

On/off switch

Terminal screw

Underwriters' knot

Socket cap

Harp

Lamp cord

Lamp nipple

Lamp base

B

REPLACING A LIGHT FIXTURE

Except for a fresh coat of paint, nothing brightens up a room more than a new light fixture. Replacement is simple since the hard work of running the house wiring has already been done.

1. Turn off the fixture's power at the main panel.

2. Remove the fixture screws and lower the fixture so it hangs by its wires.

3. The old fixture will have one white wire and one black wire—or a white wire with black tape around its end—both screwed to its terminals or connected with wire nuts. Remove the old fixture from the wires.

4. If there isn't a fixture mounting strap in place, install one (Fig. A). If there is a bare or green grounding wire in the junction box unscrew it from the box and install it under the green screw of the mounting strap.

5. Splice the new fixture wires to the house wires—black to black and white to white—using wire nuts. To splice, trim the insulation of the individual wires back $^3/_4$ inch with a wire stripper. Place the bare tips of the two wires together, insert into the wire nut, and twist the wire nut clockwise (Fig. B). Test the connections by tugging on the wires.

6. Tuck the wires into the box and fasten the new fixture with screws into the threaded holes in the fixture strap.

7. Install the light bulb(s), restore power and test the fixture.

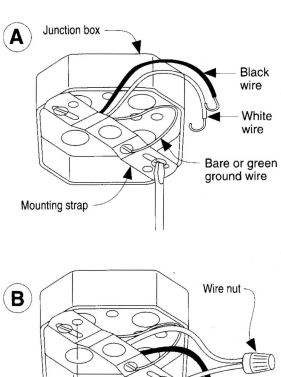

A — Junction box

Black wire

White wire

Bare or green ground wire

Mounting strap

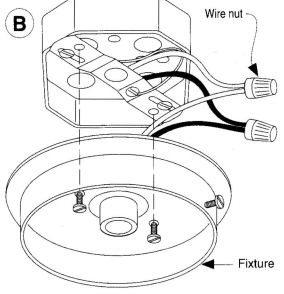

B — Wire nut

Fixture

TROUBLESHOOTING A FLUORESCENT LAMP

Several factors can cause a fluorescent lamp to act up: low room temperature, a tired bulb, a broken starter or a bad ballast. The procedure below should find the problem before you have replaced the entire fixture—which, by the way, is sometimes the best solution.

Before concluding that anything requires replacement, check that the circuit breaker is on, that the temperature of the room is at least 50°F and that the bulb is seated properly in the end sockets.

If the bulb doesn't even flicker:

• If you have a starter-type fixture (Fig. A), replace the starter. (See "Replacing a Fluorescent Starter" on page 138.)

• Replace the bulb. (See "Replacing a Fluorescent Bulb" on page 136.)

• Replace the ballast. (See "Replacing a Fluorescent Ballast" on page 140.) Check the prices before doing this; it may be as cheap or cheaper to replace the fixture!

If the bulb flickers:

• Remove the diffuser panel, remove the bulb, sand the pins and reinsert the bulb. (See "Replacing a Fluorescent Bulb" on page 136.)

• Replace the bulb. (See "Replacing a Fluorescent Bulb" on page 136.)

(continued on page 134)

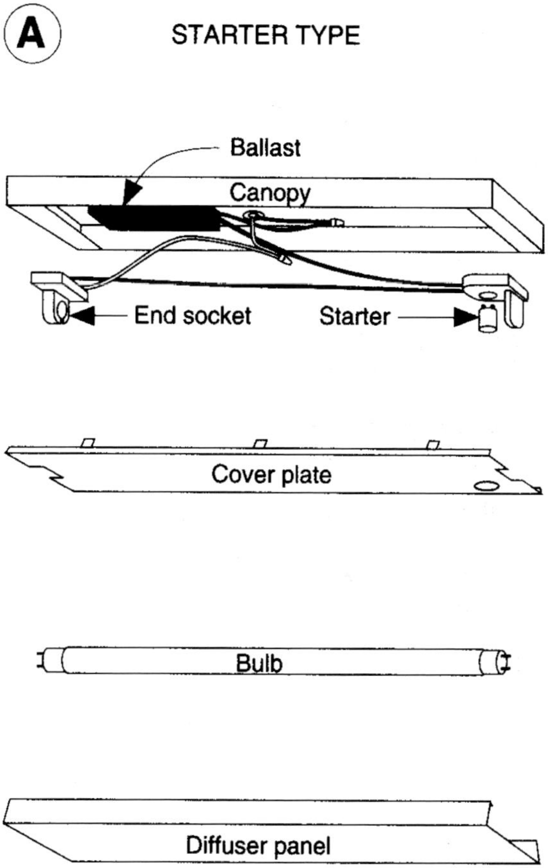

(A) STARTER TYPE

Ballast

Canopy

End socket — Starter —

Cover plate

Bulb

Diffuser panel

If the bulb is blackened:

• If the bulb is blackened only at one end, remove the bulb, turn it end-for-end, and reseat the bulb. (See "Replacing a Fluorescent Bulb" on page 136.)

• Replace both the bulb and the starter. (See "Replacing a Fluorescent Bulb" on page 136 and "Replacing a Fluorescent Starter" on page 138.)

If the bulb glows at the ends only:

• If you have a starter-type fixture (Fig. A), replace the starter. (See "Replacing a Fluorescent Starter" on page 138.)

• Replace the ballast if you think the cost is justified. (See "Replacing a Fluorescent Ballast" on page 140.)

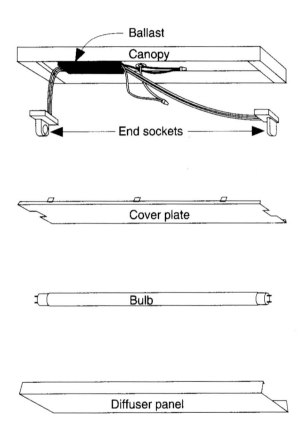

B RAPID-START TYPE (NO STARTER)

Ballast

Canopy

End sockets

Cover plate

Bulb

Diffuser panel

REPLACING A FLUORESCENT BULB

You probably already know how to change fluorescent bulbs. In case you are new to fluorescent lighting, however, here's how. Bulbs should be replaced when they burn out or begin to flicker. Spent bulbs often are black at the ends of the glass tubes.

1. Turn off the power to the light at the main panel.

2. Remove the diffuser panel—if there is one—by pulling one edge upward and away from the enclosure (Fig. A).

3. Remove the bulb by rotating it 90 degrees and pulling one end straight down. With one end free, the other end can be withdrawn.

4. Write down the type, wattage and length of the old bulb, and purchase a replacement at a home center.

5. Align the pins of the new bulb vertically with the slots in the end sockets, push the bulb straight up into the end sockets, and twist the bulb 90 degrees in either direction. You should feel the pins seat in the socket cutouts (Fig. B).

6. Replace the diffuser panel, restore power and switch on the light.

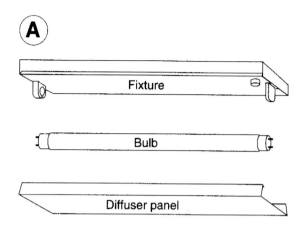

Fixture

Bulb

Diffuser panel

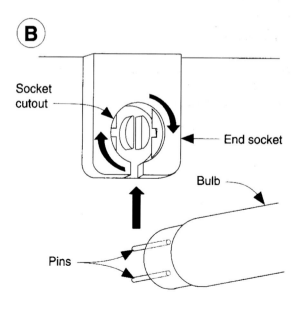

Socket cutout

End socket

Bulb

Pins

REPLACING A FLUORESCENT STARTER

Older fluorescent fixtures sometimes require starters—they look like little aluminum cans—that switch on the light when you turn on the power. Starters are so inexpensive that they are the first thing you should replace when your fluorescent light acts up. You can tell if you have starters by pulling down the diffuser panel and looking.

1. Turn off the power to the light at the main panel.

2. Remove the diffuser panel if there is one (Fig. A).

3. Remove the old starter by pressing it in and twisting counterclockwise.

4. Take the old starter to a home center or hardware store, and purchase a new one of the same type.

5. Install the new starter by inserting its contacts into the starter socket and twisting the starter clockwise (Fig. B).

6. Replace the diffuser panel, restore power and switch on the light.

138

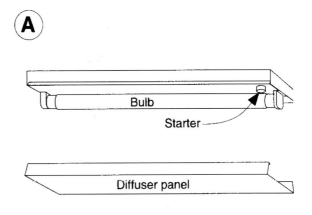

Bulb

Starter

Diffuser panel

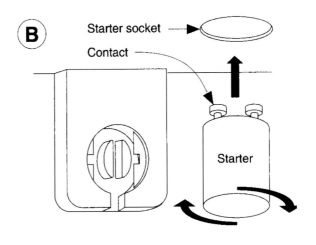

Starter socket

Contact

Starter

REPLACING A FLUORESCENT BALLAST

Fluorescent ballasts are simple to install, provided you are not afraid of stepladders. Before purchasing a replacement, however, compare the costs of a ballast and a complete fixture. The new fixture may cost even less than the ballast alone.

1. Turn off the power to the light at the main panel.

2. Remove the plastic diffuser panel (Fig. A).

3. Remove the bulb(s) by rotating 90 degrees and pulling one end straight down. (See "Replacing a Fluorescent Bulb" on page 136.)

4. Remove the cover plate by squeezing it to release the tabs on its edges from the slots in the canopy.

5. Wrap masking tape around each of the wires to the old ballast. Mark each with pairs of numbers: 1 and 1, 2 and 2, etc.

6. Disconnect any ballast wires held by wire nuts. Cut other wires at the center of the tape with diagonal cutting pliers so that each wire is numbered (Fig. B).

7. Remove the old ballast with a screwdriver and take it to a home center to buy an identical unit.

8. Install the new ballast. If earlier you cut the wires, strip the insulation from them back $1/2$ inch with a wire stripper, and connect them by inserting the bare ends of each pair of wires into a wire nut and twisting the nut clockwise (Fig. C).

9. Tuck all the wires into the canopy and replace the cover plate.

10. Replace the bulb(s) and diffuser panel, and restore power.

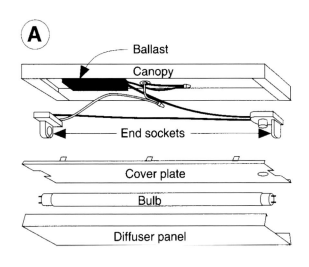

A

Ballast

Canopy

End sockets

Cover plate

Bulb

Diffuser panel

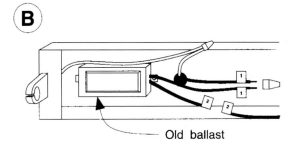

B

Old ballast

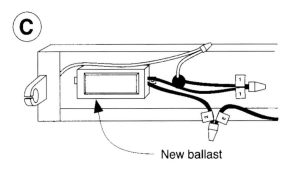

C

New ballast

APPLIANCES

FIXING A SLOW-FILLING DISHWASHER

If your automatic dishwasher fills more slowly than it did when first installed, something is clogged up. If all of your faucets run slowly, the problem could be the pipes. If just the dishwasher is slow, however, the problem is probably a clogged inlet screen.

1. Turn off the power at the main panel or, if portable, pull the plug.

2. Turn off the hot-water supply valve.

3. Remove the access panel under the loading door. It may rotate down, or you may have to remove several screws.

4. Using slip-joint pliers, unscrew the hot-water hose from the inlet valve and from the supply valve.

5. Look for a filter screen in either end of the hot-water hose. If it's not there, it will be in the inlet of the intake valve (Fig. B).

6. Label both wires and terminals on the intake valve with masking tape, then pull the wires off the terminals with long-nose pliers. If the valve inlet is hidden, use a small mirror and flashlight to look for it.

7. Carefully pry the filter screen out with a small screwdriver.

8. Clean the screen with a toothbrush and running water. If it is coated with mineral deposits, soak it in vinegar overnight.

9. Pop the screen back in and reconnect the hoses.

10. Restore the electricity and the hot water, and test for leaks. Tighten the hose couplings as necessary.

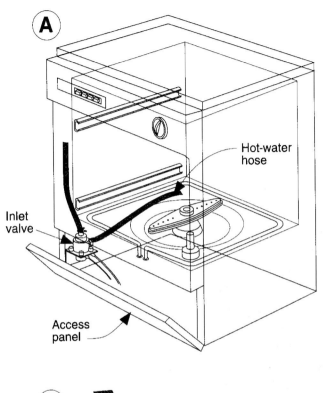

Hot-water
hose

Inlet
valve

Access
panel

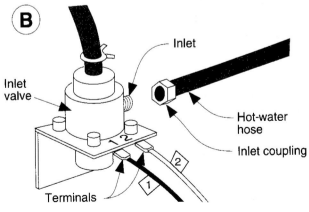

Inlet

Inlet
valve

Hot-water
hose

Inlet coupling

Terminals

REPLACING A DISHWASHER INLET VALVE

If your dishwasher fills, but too slowly, the problem is probably a clogged inlet screen. (See "Fixing a Slow-Filling Dishwasher" on page 144.) If it won't fill at all, or if it makes funny noises while filling, the problem is probably a defective inlet valve, which you can replace.

1. Turn off the power at the main panel or, if portable, pull the plug.

2. Turn off the hot-water supply valve.

3. Remove the access panel under the loading door. It may rotate down, or you may have to remove several screws.

4. Using slip-joint pliers, unscrew the hot-water hose from the inlet valve (Fig. B) and from the supply valve.

5. Using the slip-joint pliers, squeeze the fill-hose clamp, slide it up the hose, then work the hose off the intake valve.

6. Label the wires on the intake valve with masking tape, then pull the wires off the terminals with long-nose pliers.

7. Using an adjustable wrench, remove the mounting bolts and the intake valve.

8. Take the old valve to an appliance repair center and purchase a replacement.

9. Install the replacement valve in the opposite order: mounting bolts, wires, fill hose and hot-water hose.

10. Restore the electricity and the hot water, and test for leaks. Tighten the hose couplings as necessary.

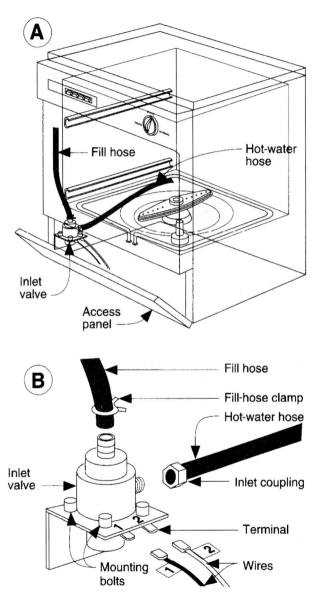

A

Fill hose

Hot-water hose

Inlet valve

Access panel

B

Fill hose

Fill-hose clamp

Hot-water hose

Inlet coupling

Inlet valve

Terminal

Mounting bolts

Wires

REPLACING A DISHWASHER FLOAT SWITCH

The float switch—located at the bottom of the dish compartment—tells the dishwasher when the compartment is empty and when it is full. If the float switch is defective or jammed, the dishwasher may either not fill or—your worst nightmare— never stop filling! Once you've cleaned up the mess, the switch is easy to check and replace.

1. Locate the float switch float inside the dishwasher (Fig. A). Check that the float moves freely by lifting it and letting it fall. If it sticks, pull the float off the stem and clean the stem with a toothbrush. Replace the float and check the operation.

2. If the dishwasher still overfills, turn the power off at the main panel, and turn off the hot water. If the dishwasher is portable, pull its plug.

3. Remove the bottom access panel to expose the float switch (Fig. B). This may require removing several screws.

4. Label the wires with masking tape, then pull the wires off the terminals with long-nose pliers.

5. Set a multitester to "R" or "Ohms."

6. Hold the multitester probes to the switch terminals and have a helper lift the float. With the float up, the multitester should read over 1,000 Ohms; down, it should read under 10 Ohms.

7. If the switch fails the test, remove the switch by removing its mounting screws, and obtain a replacement at an appliance repair center.

8. Mount the new switch, reattach the wires and replace the access panel.

9. Restore the power and the hot water.

148

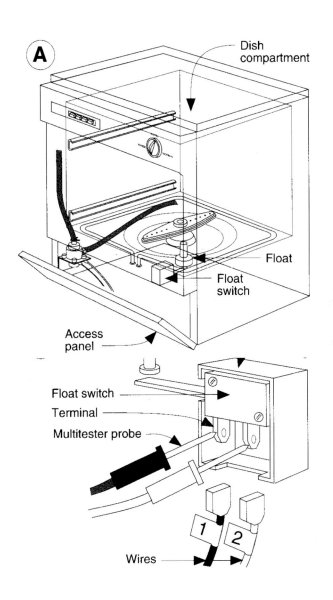

Dish compartment

Float

Float switch

Access panel

Float switch

Terminal

Multitester probe

1

2

Wires

LEVELING A CLOTHES WASHER

Does your clothes washer do the fandango? If it does hop around, the first thing to check is whether all of its feet are in contact with the floor. A washing machine on two feet is akin to a person on one foot—you wouldn't expect either to stand still for very long.

1. Place a carpenter's level on the front edge of the washer top and check the bubble (Fig. A).

2. Using an adjustable wrench, loosen the locknuts on the front leveling feet (Fig. B).

3. Use the adjustable wrench to turn the front feet until the level bubble is centered.

4. Tilt the clothes washer forward to let the self-adjusting rear feet adjust.

5. Turn the level 90 degrees to indicate front-to-back level.

6. Making identical adjustments to both, turn the front feet to center the level bubble again.

7. When the washer is level in both directions—side-to-side and front-to-back—tighten the front locknuts against the bottom of the cabinet to prevent the feet from moving.

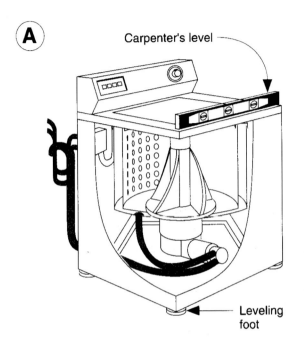

A

Carpenter's level

Leveling foot

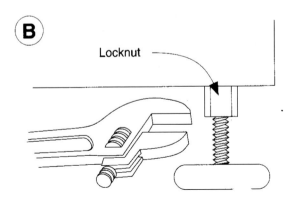

B

Locknut

REPLACING A WASHER SNUBBER

If your clothes washer sounds like someone banging on an oil drum with a baseball bat, it may be overloaded, need its feet adjusted (see "Leveling a Clothes Washer" on page 150), or it may need a new snubber. Try lighter loads and adjusting the feet first. Some new machines don't have snubbers. You can see if yours does by performing Steps 3 and 4 below.

1. Unplug the clothes washer.

2. Tape the top lid shut with duct tape.

3. Insert the blade of a putty knife under the top, 2 inches from a front corner.

4. Push the putty knife in while lifting the corner to release the top. Repeat on the other corner.

5. Raise the top and rest it against the wall behind the washer.

6. Draw a sketch of how the snubber spring rod is installed (Fig. A).

7. Lift the looped spring-rod end off the snubber.

8. Using an adjustable wrench, remove the nut and bolt that fasten the end of the snubber spring rod to the washer frame (Fig. B).

9. Using slip-joint pliers, unscrew the old snubber.

10. Remove the snubber spring rod. Take the rod and snubber to an appliance repair center and purchase replacements.

11. Screw the new snubber in, install the new spring rod and snap the spring rod over the snubber.

12. Close the lid, remove the duct tape and plug the clothes washer in.

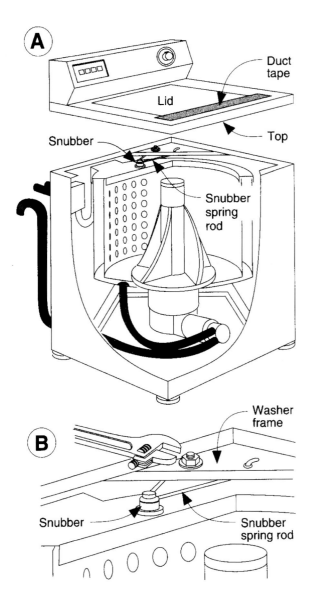

Duct
tape

Lid

Top

Snubber

Snubber
spring
rod

Washer
frame

Snubber

Snubber
spring rod

FIXING A SLOW-FILLING CLOTHES WASHER

*If your automatic clothes washer fills more slowly
than it did when new, something is clogged up.
If all of your faucets run slowly, the problem
could be the pipes. If just the clothes washer is
slow, however, the problem is probably nothing
more complicated than clogged inlet screens.*

1. Unplug the clothes washer.

2. Pull the washer away from the wall to gain access.

3. If there is any question, use masking tape to mark
the hoses "hot" and "cold."

4. Shut off both water supply valves.

5. Using slip-joint pliers, loosen the hose couplings
at the machine, then unscrew and remove them
(Fig. A).

6. Inlet screens should be visible inside the
machine inlets. Pry the screens out with a small
screwdriver, trying not to puncture them (Fig. B). If
you damage the screens, you can purchase new
ones at an appliance repair center.

7. Clean the screens with an old toothbrush and running water. If the screens are coated with a mineral
deposit, soak them in a cup of vinegar overnight.

8. Push the screens back into the machine inlets
with the convex—dome-shaped—side facing out.

9. Reinstall the hot- and cold-water hoses hand tight,
then take another $1/4$ turn with the slip-joint pliers.

10. Push the clothes washer back into place and
restore the power.

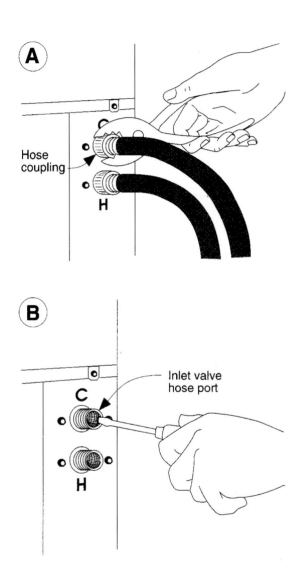

Hose
coupling

Inlet valve
hose port

FIXING AN OVERFLOWING CLOTHES WASHER

If your clothes washer fills and fills and fills—turn off the supply valves! After you have cleaned up the mess, check the level switch that is designed to tell the machine when it is full enough. Either the plastic pressure hose has fallen off or you need to replace the switch.

1. Unplug the clothes washer.

2. Remove the screws fastening the console to the end caps.

3. Pull the console up and back, and let it rest on its hinges.

4. Label the three wires of the level switch with tape, then pull the wires off, using long-nose pliers (Fig. A).

5. Remove the pressure hose from the level switch and slip a 2-foot length of $1/4$-inch plastic tubing over the port (Fig. B).

6. Set a multitester to "Ohms" and place the probes on the two outside terminals of the level switch (Fig. C).

7. With the probes in place, have a helper blow on the end of the tubing. If the multitester reading doesn't drop to less than 10 Ohms, take the switch to an appliance repair center for a replacement.

8. Connect the pressure hose to the pressure port and the three wires to the matching terminals of the new switch.

9. Lower the console into position and fasten it to the end caps with the screws you removed earlier.

10. Plug the washer in and run it. Stand by to abort the first fill cycle, since the pressure tube may send a false signal the first time.

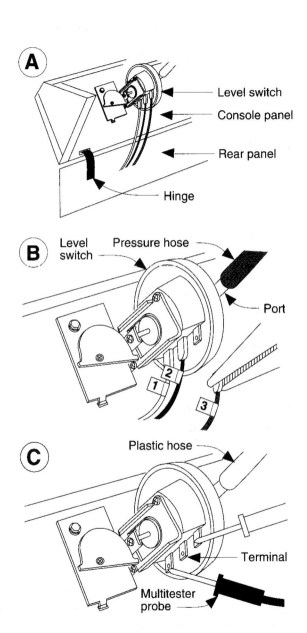

A
Level switch
Console panel
Rear panel
Hinge

B
Level switch
Pressure hose
Port
1
2
3

C
Plastic hose
Terminal
Multitester probe

REPLACING A WASHER INLET VALVE

If your clothes washer fills, but too slowly, the problem is probably a clogged inlet screen. (See "Fixing a Slow-Filling Clothes Washer" on page 154.) If it won't fill at all, or if it makes funny noises while filling, the problem may be a defective inlet valve, which you can easily replace.

1. Unplug the clothes washer.

2. Shut off both hot- and cold-water supply valves.

3. Using slip-joint pliers, loosen and then remove the supply hoses at the rear of the machine (Fig. A).

4. Tape the top lid shut with duct tape.

5. Insert a putty knife under the top, 2 inches from a corner, push the putty knife in, and lift the corner (Fig. B). Repeat at the other corner and swing the top up.

6. Using a nut driver, remove the screws fastening the inlet valve to the rear panel and remove the valve (Fig. C, page 160).

7. The valve will have 1, 2 or 3 pairs of wires, each pair feeding a coil. Label each of the wires and its corresponding terminal with masking tape, then pull the connectors off the terminals.

8. Set a multitester to "Ohms" and place its two probes on each pair of valve terminals (Fig. D, page160). If the tester reads less than 10 or more than 1,000 Ohms on any pair of terminals, it must be replaced.

(continued on page 160)

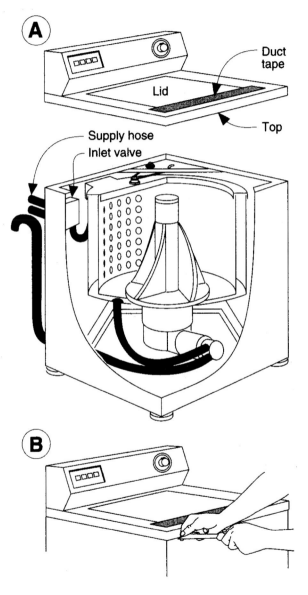

A

Duct tape

Lid

Top

Supply hose

Inlet valve

B

9. Using the slip-joint pliers, pinch the clamp holding the inlet hose on the inlet valve, slide the clamp down the hose and work the hose off the valve.

10. Take the inlet valve to an appliance repair center and purchase a replacement.

11. Work the end of the inlet hose over the outlet port of the new inlet valve.

12. Squeeze the ends of the hose clamp with the slip-joint pliers and work the clamp up over the outlet port to clamp the hose in place.

13. Push the wire connectors over the corresponding terminals of the new valve.

14. Insert the hot and cold ports of the inlet valve through the holes in the rear panel of the washer and fasten the valve with the screws removed earlier.

15. Attach the hot and cold supply hoses hand tight, then tighten the couplings $^1/_4$ turn farther, using the slip-joint pliers.

16. Replace the power plug and move the machine back in place.

17. Turn on the hot- and cold-water supply valves, and remove the duct tape from the lid.

18. Run the clothes washer through a wash cycle to test for leaks. Tighten the supply-hose couplings as necessary.

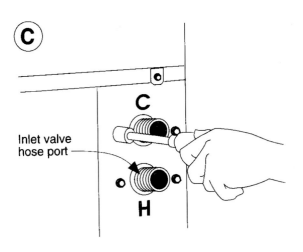

C

Inlet valve hose port

H

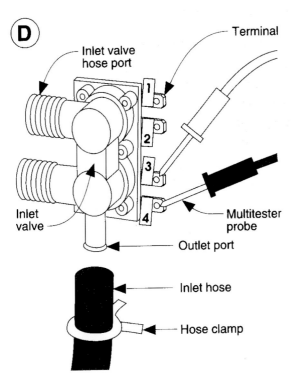

Inlet valve hose port

Terminal

1

2

3

Inlet valve

4

Multitester probe

Outlet port

Inlet hose

Hose clamp

WINTERIZING A CLOTHES WASHER

Do you have a clothes washer at a summer camp? If so, don't just lock the doors and leave it for the winter. Water in the inlet valve and pump can freeze and crack the valve and pump bodies. All you need to protect the machine is a quart of non-toxic— "RV"—antifreeze. Jack Daniels works as well but costs four times as much.

1. Turn off both water supply valves.

2. Turn the timer control knob to "Fill" and the temperature selection knob to "Warm Wash" (Fig. A).

3. Turn the machine on for 10 seconds.

4. Unplug the washer and pull it away from the wall to gain rear access.

5. Using slip-joint pliers, loosen the hose couplings at the machine, then unscrew and remove them (Fig. B).

6. Lift the lid and pour 1 quart of non-toxic antifreeze—propylene glycol—into the machine.

7. Plug in the machine.

8. Turn the washer timer control to "Drain and Spin," and let the machine run for 10 seconds.

9. The washer is now freeze-proof. To use the machine again, hook up the supply hoses, pour 1 cup of liquid clothes-washing detergent into the machine and run the machine through a complete wash/rinse/spin cycle.

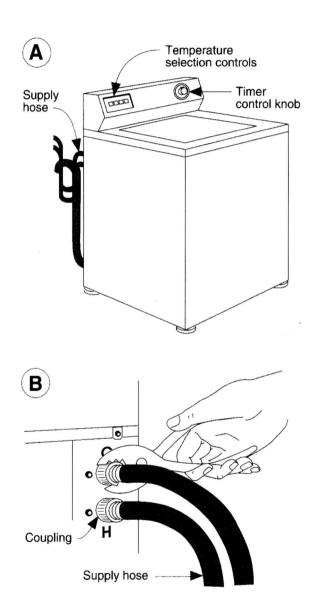

A

Temperature
selection controls

Supply
hose

Timer
control knob

B

Coupling

H

Supply hose

REPLACING A DRYER LIGHT BULB

Do you need a flashlight to see what is in your clothes dryer? If so, the drum light has probably burned out. Some of the less expensive models have no light, but it is as simple as opening the door and looking to find out. The bulb is an ordinary household bulb of 25 to 40 watts.

1. Turn off the power at the main panel or unplug the dryer.

2. Open the loading door and locate the white plastic light cover at the rear (Fig. A).

3. Twist the plastic cover clockwise to release and remove the cover (Fig. B). If the cover will not turn, try twisting it clockwise.

4. Unscrew the light bulb counterclockwise and remove it.

5. Replace the bulb with one of the same or lower wattage. In any case, do not exceed 40 watts.

6. Line up the tabs of the cover with the slots in the lamp socket and twist the cover counterclockwise to engage the tabs.

7. Restore power and confirm that the lamp lights when the dryer door is opened.

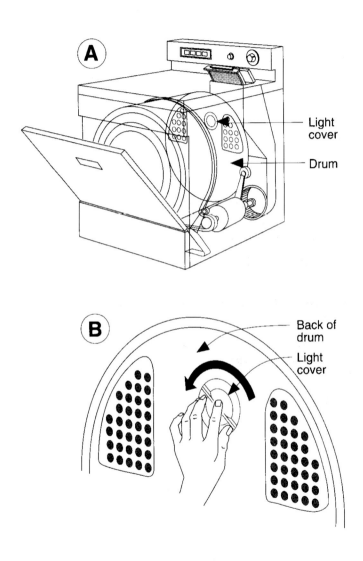

A

Light cover

Drum

B

Back of drum

Light cover

CLEANING A DRYER VENT

Residential energy audits have shown that over 90 percent of clothes-dryer exhaust ducts and hoods have significant deposits of lint. The lint restricts the exhaust airflow and makes the dryer less efficient. Worse, an exhaust damper stuck open admits cold air in winter.

1. Unplug the dryer. If the dryer is gas, turn off the gas supply valve, too.

2. Pull the dryer out to expose rear panel (Fig. A). If gas, be careful not to kink the gas supply tubing.

3. Remove the duct from the outlet at the rear panel and from the exhaust hood where it exits the building. If the duct is a plastic hose, you'll need to loosen the hose clamps at each end with a screwdriver first. If the duct is metal, you may have to remove duct tape from the joints.

4. Use a toothbrush to remove the lint from the dryer outlet and from the flapper of the exhaust hood (Fig. B).

5. Feed string through the entire length of the duct. You may have to remove duct tape from the joints and separate the duct into shorter sections.

6. With the string, tie a knot at the midpoint of a hand towel (Fig. C).

7. Pull the towel through the duct to remove the lint.

8. Retape any joints you disconnected.

9. Reconnect the duct ends to the dryer and the exhaust hood.

10. Restore the power—and gas—and carefully push the dryer back in place.

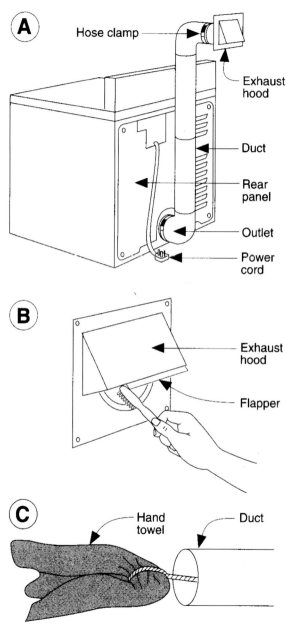

A Hose clamp — Exhaust hood — Duct — Rear panel — Outlet — Power cord

B Exhaust hood — Flapper

C Hand towel — Duct

Replacing a Dryer Timer

Symptoms of a defective clothes-dryer timer are a dryer that will not start or that stops in the middle of a cycle. If the timer is working, the timer knob should move—though watching it is somewhat like watching grass grow. If the dryer still doesn't run after replacing the timer, the likely cause is either the door switch or the start switch.

1. Unplug the dryer.

2. Remove the timer knob by pulling it toward you (Fig. A).

3. Using a screwdriver, remove the screws that fasten the console to the end caps. The screws may be either in the sides or the front of the end cap.

4. Lay the console down on the top of the cabinet.

5. If they are not already marked, label each wire with masking tape to avoid confusion when connecting the wires to the new timer.

6. Pull each wire off its terminal, using long-nose pliers (Fig. B).

7. Using a nut driver, remove the screws that fasten the timer (Fig. C).

8. Take the timer to an appliance repair center and purchase an exact replacement.

9. Fasten the replacement timer with the nut driver and screws.

10. Push each labeled wire onto its corresponding terminal.

11. Fasten the console to the end caps, push the timer knob back on and plug the dryer in.

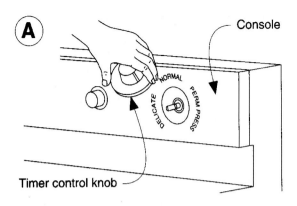

Console

Timer control knob

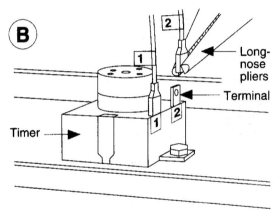

Long-nose pliers

Terminal

Timer

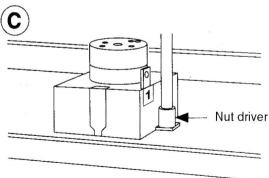

Nut driver

REPLACING A DRYER BELT

The belt that turns the drum is usually the first thing to go on a clothes dryer. The clue to a broken belt is that the dryer will make all of its normal noises, but the drum will not turn. It may seem that you have totally disassembled the dryer by the time you get to the belt, but the procedure for replacement is simple and straightforward.

1. Unplug the dryer. If it is a gas dryer, turn off the gas supply as well.

2. If the lint filter is located in the top of the dryer, pull it out of its slot (Fig. A).

3. Using a screwdriver, remove the two screws in front of the filter slot (Fig. B).

4. Slip the blade of a putty knife between the top and front of the machine, 2 inches in from a corner (Fig. C, page 173). Push in on the putty knife while lifting the top to release the clip. Repeat at the other front corner.

5. Lift the top—it hinges at the rear—and rest it against the wall.

6. Slip the putty knife between the access panel and door bottom at the midpoint. Push in on the putty knife while pulling one of the top corners of the toe panel toward you until the toe panel opens.

7. Tape the door closed with duct tape.

8. If there are wires connected to a door switch on the inside of the front panel, label the wires and the terminals with masking tape, then remove the wires with long-nose pliers. Remove any clips that secure the wires to the front panel.

(continued on page 172)

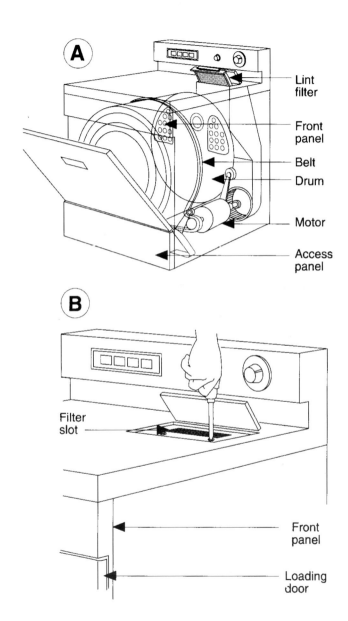

A

Lint filter

Front panel

Belt

Drum

Motor

Access panel

B

Filter slot

Front panel

Loading door

9. Using either a screwdriver or a nut driver, loosen—but do not remove—the 2 screws at the bottom of the front panel.

10. Have a helper hold up the front of the dryer drum while you remove the two screws inside the top of the front panel.

11. Remove the bottom screws loosened earlier and remove the front panel. Lower the drum.

12. Note how the old belt loops around the drum, the motor pulley and the idler pulley so you won't be confused when you install the new belt.

13. Push the idler pulley toward the motor (Fig. E) and remove the drive belt from the motor pulley and drum.

14. Take the old belt to an appliance repair center and purchase a replacement.

15. Place the new belt around the drum with the ribbed surface on the drum.

16. Feed the belt under the idler pulley and, while pushing the idler pulley toward the motor, slip the belt around the motor pulley.

17. With a helper holding the front of the drum up, replace the front panel.

18. Reconnect the front panel wires.

19. Replace the toe panel.

20. Replace the top panel.

21. Replace the screws in front of the lint filter slot and the lint filter.

22. Restore the power and the gas.

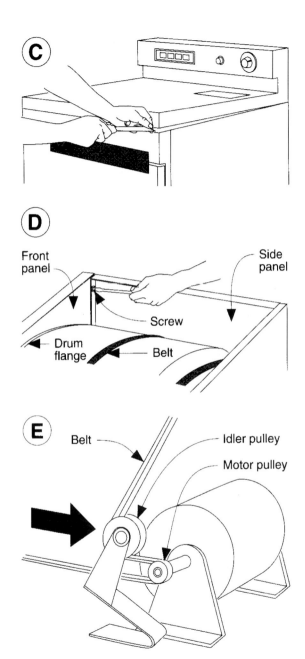

C

D

Front panel

Side panel

Screw

Drum flange

Belt

E

Belt

Idler pulley

Motor pulley

REPLACING A SURFACE ELEMENT

There is no reason to suffer the inconvenience of a cold or lukewarm electric-stove surface element. First, you can tell if one is broken simply by switching it with a working element. Second, you can purchase replacements at most hardware stores.

1. Determine which of the range's surface elements do and do not work.

2. Turn off all of the surface controls (Fig. A) and let the elements cool.

3. Switch the element you suspect is defective with a working element. The elements sit on supports and are plugged into two-prong receptacles. To remove an element, lift the element from its support and pull its prongs straight back out of the receptacle (Fig. B).

4. Turn on the two switched elements.

5. If the previously suspect element now works, the problem is in the wiring of the range or the element control—not in the element. Call an appliance repair service.

6. If the suspect element does not work in the second receptacle, the element is bad and must be replaced.

7. Take the bad element to an appliance repair center and purchase a replacement.

8. Plug the prongs of the replacement element into the receptacle and seat the element on its support.

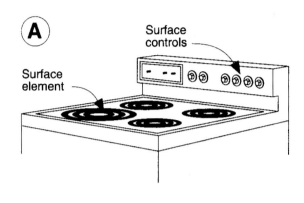

A

Surface controls

Surface element

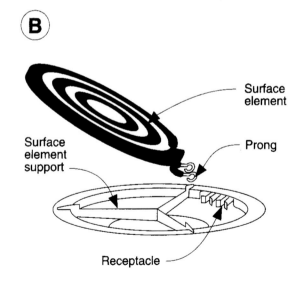

B

Surface element

Surface element support

Prong

Receptacle

REPLACING AN OVEN ELEMENT

Have you been living without home-baked cookies because your oven doesn't work? By switching the upper and lower elements, you can tell if either one is defective. If one proves defective, you should be able to get replacement elements at your appliance dealer or an appliance repair center.

1. Turn the oven control to "Bake" and observe if the lower element is working.

2. Turn the oven control to "Broil" and observe if the upper element is working.

3. If neither element is working, the problem is most likely in the range wiring or oven control; call a professional repair service. If one is working but not the other, continue.

4. If the elements are identical, switch them. To remove an element, turn off the power at the main panel, remove the screws of the element bracket (Fig. B), and pull the element out to expose the wires. Use a screwdriver or nut driver to remove the wires from the element terminals (Fig. C).

5. Restore power and repeat Steps 1 and 2. If the suspect element now works and the formerly working element doesn't, the problem is in the wiring or controls; call a repair service. If the suspect element is still not working, the element is bad.

6. Turn the power off, take the bad element to an appliance repair center and purchase a replacement.

7. Reattach the element prongs to the supply terminals and remount the element support bracket.

8. Turn the power back on.

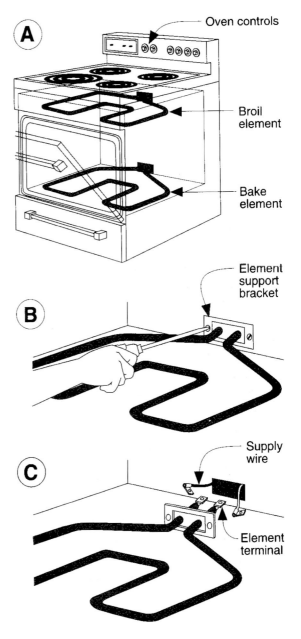

A Oven controls

Broil element

Bake element

B Element support bracket

C Supply wire

Element terminal

MAKING A REFRIGERATOR DOOR CLOSE

Because of teenagers, refrigerator and freezer doors are designed to close automatically. After all, you can't expect persons preoccupied with life's truly important issues to obsess about such little things as utility bills. If you often find your refrigerator door standing open, here is what to do about it—other than giving the kids away.

1. Place a carpenter's level side-to-side on top of the refrigerator.

2. Using an adjustable wrench or slip-joint pliers, turn the leveling feet at the front corners to center the level bubble.

3. Adjust the rear feet until both touch the floor.

4. Turn the level 90 degrees so that it lines up with a side of the refrigerator top.

5. Making identical adjustments to both, turn the front feet to center the level bubble again.

6. Open the door slightly. If it stays put or closes, you are done. If it opens further, continue.

7. Using a screwdriver, pry the cover—if there is one—off the top door hinge.

8. Using a nut driver, slightly loosen the screws of both the top and middle hinges. If the refrigerator has a single door, loosen only the top hinge screws.

9. With the door(s) closed, line the door(s) up with the sides of the refrigerator (and each other).

10. Tighten the screws and close the door(s) to check the alignment. If necessary, repeat Steps 8 through 10.

11. Replace the hinge cover.

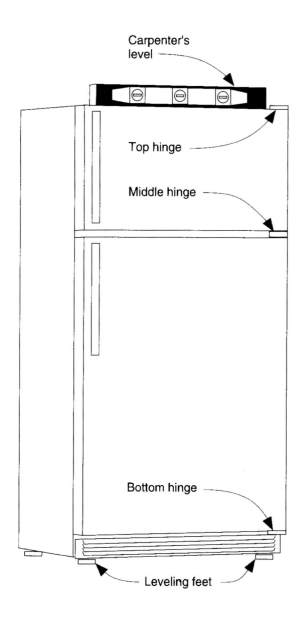

Carpenter's level

Top hinge

Middle hinge

Bottom hinge

Leveling feet

CLEANING REFRIGERATOR COILS

If your refrigerator seems to be laboring overtime lately, the problem may be dust on the condenser coils. The condenser dissipates the heat pumped out of the refrigerator box. Dust on the coils and fins acts as insulation, preventing the heat from dissipating. Clean the coils once per year.

If the refrigerator has tubing on the back:

1. Pull the refrigerator out so you can get at the back. You may have to unplug it for a few minutes.

2. Using a vacuum cleaner with a brush attachment, loosen and vacuum up the lint and dirt from the tubing and fins. If you don't have a vacuum cleaner with a brush, use a paint brush.

3. Return the refrigerator.

If there is no tubing:

1. Unplug the refrigerator.

2. Open the lower refrigerator door and prop it open.

3. Hold the motor compartment grille at both ends, push it down, and rotate the top toward you. If the top does not release, look for projecting tabs that will release the grille. Lift the grille off its bottom supports and set it aside.

4. While a helper shines a light into the motor compartment, vacuum or brush the condenser.

5. Clean the condenser fan with a toothbrush.

6. Replace the motor compartment grille and plug the refrigerator in.

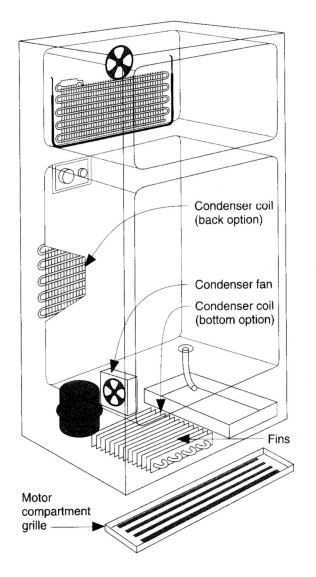

Condenser coil
(back option)

Condenser fan

Condenser coil
(bottom option)

Fins

Motor
compartment
grille

REPLACING A DEFROST COIL

Does your automatic-defrost freezer resemble a glacier? If the answer is "yes," the reason may be a burned-out defrost heater. If you have a multitester, you can easily determine whether the defrost heater needs replacing. If you don't have a multitester, live with the glacier or call the repair service.

1. Unplug the refrigerator.

2. Clean out the freezer compartment (Fig. A). Place frozen food you wish to keep frozen in a cooler.

3. Using a screwdriver, remove the screws securing the evaporator cover. You may have to remove shelves and shelf supports as well.

4. Remove the evaporator cover, exposing the evaporator coil and the U-shaped defrost heater that wraps around the perimeter of the coil.

5. Disconnect the ends of the defrost heater from their supply wires.

6. Set a multitester to "Ohms."

7. Touch the two multitester probes to the two ends of the defrost heater (Fig. B). The meter should read between 10 and 1,000 Ohms. If not, the heater is bad and must be replaced.

8. From the back of the refrigerator, record the manufacturer and model of the refrigerator. With that information, purchase a replacement defrost heater from an appliance repair center.

9. Remove and replace the defrost heater, connect the wires and replace the evaporator cover.

182

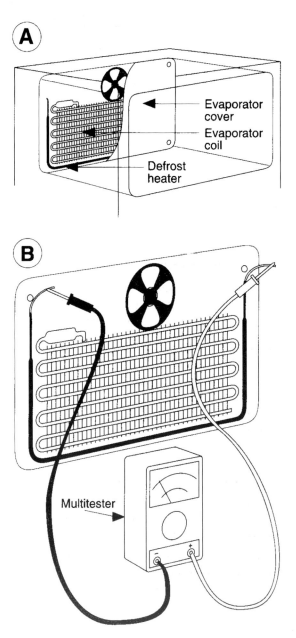

Evaporator
cover

Evaporator
coil

Defrost
heater

Multitester

TOUCHING UP APPLIANCE SCRATCHES

A scratched or scuffed finish on an appliance will not affect the performance of the appliance, but it may detract from the appearance of the kitchen you just spent $10,000 remodeling. A can of touch-up paint will cost no more than $10. If the appliance is white, you can obtain "appliance white" gloss enamel at any hardware store.

Wash the surface to be painted with a kitchen scrub pad and household detergent. Rinse with fresh water and dry.

If the scratch is small (Fig. A):

1. Obtain a $1/2$-ounce touch-up bottle of paint at an appliance repair center.

2. Fill the scratch with the smallest amount of paint possible.

If the scratched area is large (Fig. B):

1. Obtain a 15-ounce spray can of matching paint at an appliance repair center.

2. Lightly sand the area to be painted with 600-grit sandpaper.

3. Wipe the area with a damp cloth and let it dry.

4. Shake the spray can according to the directions on the can.

5. Spray the entire area very lightly and let it dry.

6. Repeat Step 5 until the sprayed area looks the same as the surrounding area. This will require several applications. Resist the urge to spray thick coats. Heavy applications will result in a wavy appearance.

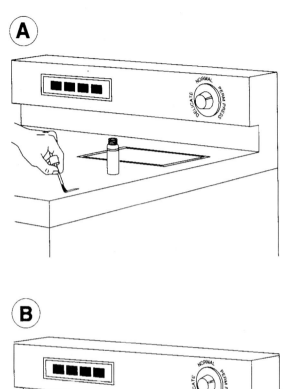

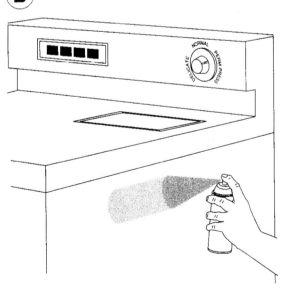